Table of Contents

1. An Introduction to Trade 2

2. What Is Trade? 4
    The Lemonade Stand 4
    Goods and Services 6
    Why Do We Trade? 6
    How Do We Trade? 6
    How Are Trade Items Valued? 6
    The Importance of Trade 8

3. A Brief History of Trade 10

4. Early Trade in Canada 14
    The Hudson's Bay Company 15
    The North West Company 16
    The Decline of the Fur Trade 16
    Manufacturing Comes to Canada 17

5. What Is an Export? 18
    Main Reasons to Export 20
    Canadian Exports 21
    Natural Resources 22
    Fresh Water 23

6. What Is an Import? 24
    Main Reasons to Import 24
    Import to Export? Crazy Trading! 25
    Canadian Imports 26

7. Canada's Trading Partners 29
    The United States, Japan,
        Britain, Mexico 29
    Europe 30
    Asia 31
    South America 32
    Africa 33
    Oceania 34

8. Global Connections 36

9. Time Zones 38

10. The US: A Closer Look 40
    Northeastern Region 42
    Midwestern Region 44
    Southern Region 46
    Western Region 48

11. Trading with the US 50
    NAFTA 50
    Dependency on the United States 50
    What Is Traded? 52
    Why Do We Buy American? 52

12. Japan: A Closer Look 54
    Landforms and Climate 54
    Political Facts 56
    Social Facts 56
    Japan's Economy 58

13. Mexico: A Closer Look 60
    Landforms and Climate 60
    Political Facts 62
    Social Facts 62
    Mexico's Economy 64
    NAFTA 65

14. Insights into Production 66

15. Canadians on the World Stage 68
    Donovan Bailey 68
    Claudia Bertrand 68
    Roberta Bondar 68
    Wesley Chu 69
    Celine Dion 69
    Karen Kain 70
    Craig Kielburger 70
    Keith Peiris 70
    David Suzuki 71
    Morgan Long 71

16. International Trade Groups 72
    Trade Organizations 72
    Trade Agreements 73
    Canada and International Trade 73
    The World Trade Organization 74
    The Organization for Economic
        Cooperation and Development 74
    Asia Pacific Economic Cooperation 75
    The Commonwealth 75
    La Francophonie 75
    Organization of American States 75

17. Peacekeeping 76
    Canada's Peacekeeping Missions 76
    Problems in Peacekeeping 76

All terms appearing in bold face type in the text are defined in the Glossary that appears on pages 78–79.

*L*ee is connected to the world in many ways because Canada trades with many countries. We trade when we buy, sell, or exchange **goods**.

Goods are things that we need or want. Goods we need are those basic items that we have to have in order to survive. Goods we want are those things that bring us pleasure or make our lives easier. But we don't need them in order to survive and grow.

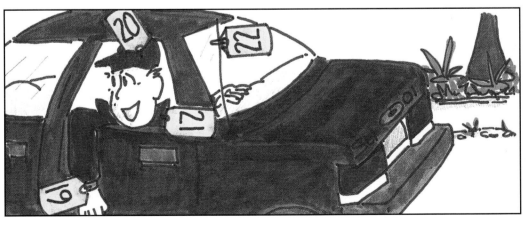

SOMETHING TO DO

1. Can you identify Lee's **needs** and **wants**?

LEGEND

1. Made in Korea.
2. Made in Singapore.
3. Made in China.
4. Made in Canada.
5. Made in U.S.A.
6. Made in Korea.
7. Made in U.S.A.
8. Made in France.
9. Made in Japan.
10. Made in Canada.
11. Made in Canada.
12. Made in Japan.
13. Made in U.S.A.
14. Made in Canada
15. Made in Columbia.
16. Made in U.S.A.
17. Made in Mexico.
18. Made in Scotland.
19. Made in England.
20. Made in U.S.A.
21. Made in China.
22. Made in Japan.

renden plopped himself down under the nearest tree, turned to his best friend and sighed, "I can't believe how hot it is! I can't ever remember it being so hot."

It was four weeks into summer vacation. It was hot and muggy, and Brenden and David were BORED!

"I'm thirsty," said Brenden. "Let's get something to drink."

"Okay," agreed David. Although David wasn't really thirsty, he thought maybe a trip into the house might help pass the time.

Pulling open the back door, the boys saw Brenden's younger sister sprawled on the kitchen floor, crayons scattered about.

The boys made their way to the refrigerator, stepping over Hannah as they went. Hannah continued to colour, not seeming to notice them.

"What are you colouring?" asked Brenden.

"I'm making signs for a lemonade stand," answered Hannah.

Hannah turned to the boys, with a sparkle in her eyes. "Would you help me? Dad said he would make the lemonade as soon as he was finished reading to Brian, but it's been a long time. Would you make the lemonade?"

There was silence. Several moments passed. Hannah was just about to repeat the question when Brenden looked over and said, "Okay. I guess so." He looked at David and smiled, "We *are* thirsty." Then without hesitation, he went to get a pitcher.

"Oh!...wait a minute," said Hannah. "Who gets to keep the money?"

Brenden stopped in his tracks. "Um...well...there are three of us, so you can have a third of the money as well as all the drinks you want. Sound fair?"

"It's a deal!" said Hannah.

Brenden fetched the pitcher out of the cupboard, found the tin of lemonade, and went about searching for a spoon. Together they assembled the ingredients and then made their way out the back door. "Wait a minute," said David. "We don't have any cups."

"Hang on. I'll get them." Brenden went back into the kitchen but returned, empty-handed. "I can't find any plastic cups. Now what are we going to do?"

"I guess we..." Hannah's sentence was interrupted when the back door swung open and Hannah's dad appeared. "So how about I make that lemonade now?" he asked.

"Already done, Dad. Brenden and David helped me. We were going to split the money three ways, but now we can't find any cups."

"Well, I think I know where there might be some." He stepped back into the kitchen, then suddenly stopped and turned to the kids. With a chuckle he said, "So does this mean I'm a partner, too?"

"I guess we could split it four ways—or you could have the first drink, Dad," replied Brenden.

"No thanks. It's okay. But I know what I will take in exchange for the cups. I want a promise that everything gets put away when you're finished." With a quick exchange of glances, it was decided. They agreed to the deal and headed out the door with lemonade, cups, and signs in hand. On such a hot day, who knows how much lemonade they might sell!

More than likely Brenden, Hannah, and David had a very profitable day. What made the whole idea work was their willingness to exchange goods and services among themselves.

SOMETHING TO DO

1. Conduct a survey in your class to determine how much students are willing to pay for a glass of lemonade. Based on the results, what would be a reasonable price to charge?

2. Create an advertisement for a lemonade stand.

GOODS AND SERVICES

You just learned that trade occurs when we buy, sell, or exchange goods. Goods are the things we need or want, such as food and water and computers and snowboards.

Trade can also happen when we buy, sell, or exchange **services**. When a person does a job for someone, he or she is providing a service.

Hannah performed a service when she created the signs for the lemonade stand. Brenden and David performed a service when they made the goods (the lemonade). Their dad also provided goods (the cups). In exchange for their goods and services, the group made money. In exchange for his goods, their dad made the group promise to perform the service of cleaning when they were finished.

WHY DO WE TRADE?

- We have more of an item than we need. We have a **surplus**, so we sell or exchange it for something we need or want.
- We don't have an item. We then have to buy it from someone else.

HOW DO WE TRADE?

Imagine a situation where you and another student exchange one trading card for another. That is a direct exchange of goods. When goods are simply traded for other goods, it is called **bartering**. In the past, bartering was a necessary way of life in order to survive and obtain items you needed.

Bartering requires two people, and each person has to have goods and services that the other wants. It is not always a practical way of trading. A farmer may have excess food and want to trade it for tools. He would need to find someone who has excess tools and needs food.

Money has made trading a lot easier. Money means trading doesn't need to be a direct exchange of goods or services. A farmer can find one person who needs his food, and in exchange, he will receive money. He could then use that money to purchase tools from another person, such as a toolmaker.

It takes at least two people for a trade to occur. Trade can also happen between groups of people or whole countries. Trade that happens between people in the same country is referred to as **domestic trade**. Trade that happens between people in different countries is referred to as **international trade**.

HOW ARE TRADE ITEMS VALUED?

In order for a trade to take place, Hannah must have wanted the service (making lemonade) the boys could provide. In exchange for the boys' service, she was willing to give

Trade may involve the direct exchange of one good or service for another.

Food ⟷ Tools = Bartering (2 people)

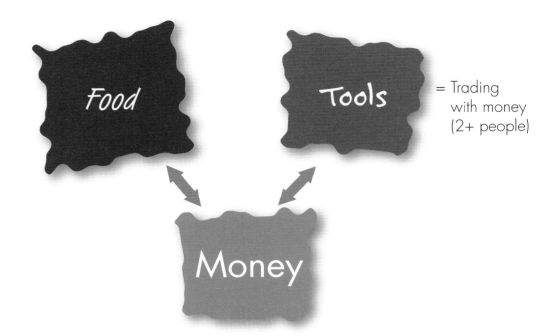

Food   Tools   = Trading with money (2+ people)

Money

up some of the **profits**. The profits are the amount of money the group earned after they subtracted what it cost to make the lemonade. Their costs might have included buying the lemonade mix.

A trade will take place only if both people involved in the trade value the services or goods they are going to receive.

How do we decide which goods or services are more valuable? Usually, **supply and demand** determine the value. Think about trading cards. What would happen if only a certain number of cards were printed? The supply of trading cards would be limited and not everyone would be able to purchase a card. The card would become hard to get, and therefore more valuable. It would sell for a higher price because it would be rare and many people would want it (it would be in demand).

On the other hand, what would happen if there were many copies of the same card printed? The copies would be easy to get, and they would not be as valuable. There would be little demand because everyone could easily purchase the card.

SOMETHING TO DO

1. What cards, beads, toys, magazines, or other items do you collect and/or trade? Interview students in your class to find out what they collect and what they trade. You might ask them if they have any trading secrets to share. To help you collect and analyze the data, create a survey chart and record results as you interview your classmates.

Name	Trading Items	Trading Secrets

THE IMPORTANCE OF TRADE

When we trade, we can buy some of the things we need or want from others. Can you imagine what your life would be like if you had to make everything you needed or wanted, from food to toys? Because we don't have to make everything on our own, we can focus on making one thing and become very good at it. For example, your father or mother can focus on making a car at the automobile factory, while someone else can concentrate on growing vegetables. If we focus on a particular job such as making cars, then we can sell the service to others who need it.

Trading allows factories or companies to focus on making **products**, such as computer games. The company can hire skilled workers and buy special equipment, which helps to make the job easier. Making the job easier means the company can create more of the product. It can then sell the product at a lower cost. This lower cost is passed on to **consumers**, or buyers, who will have more money to buy more products.

Trade allows people to specialize in jobs and companies to specialize in products. It also allows countries to specialize in goods and services.

Most goods can be categorized in one of two ways: as **raw materials** or **manufactured consumer goods**. Raw materials are things in their natural form that have not been changed to make other products. Manufactured consumer goods are products that have been made by hand or machine.

Each country is unique and has certain raw materials that it can sell to other countries or use itself to produce manufactured consumer goods. When a country focuses on producing certain goods, it can create enough of those goods to sell to other countries around the world.

Trade is an important part of every country's **economy**, or wealth. A country may be considered wealthy, depending on the number of goods it has and the money it has. To decide how wealthy you are, you might look at the number of toys you have and at the amount of money in your bank account!

The exchanging of goods and services creates jobs, helps meet the wants and needs of the people, and brings money into a country.

The wheat many Canadian farmers grow is a raw material. What are some other raw materials found in Canada?

The computer games you and your friends play are manufactured consumer goods. What other consumer goods do you use regularly?

SOMETHING TO DO

1. List three reasons why trade is important.

2. Start a personal dictionary of key words. Add any new words to your dictionary as you encounter them.

   a) Divide your notebook page into two columns. Make the column on the left narrower than the column on the right. Write the title "Word" in the column on the left and the title "Meaning" in the column on the right.

   b) In the left column, write the key word. In the right column, write the meaning of the word or draw a sketch of it. Try to write the definition in your own words.

   Start your dictionary with the following words:

   trade   goods   services   supply and demand   profit   raw materials

3. Estimate the profits you might make on a daily basis and a weekly basis if you set up a lemonade stand in your area.

   a) Use a grocery store flyer to estimate the cost of making the lemonade. Consider the cost of the lemonade mix, the disposable cups, and the bottled water. Based on the estimated costs, what would be a reasonable amount to charge for a cup of lemonade?

   b) Now that you know the cost of making and selling the lemonade and have decided on the price to charge your customers, estimate your profits. Don't forget to consider factors that might increase or reduce sales, such as sunny days or cold and rainy days.

hen do you think the very first trade took place? What do you think was traded?

We know that for thousands of years people hunted for their own food and created their own simple tools. They also made any clothes they needed. In **nomadic** groups, they travelled continuously in search of food and fresh pasture for their animals.

DID YOU KNOW?

Have you ever heard of the expression "to buy a pig in a poke"? Long ago farmers would bring pigs to the market in a poke or small sack. Sometimes a dishonest farmer might put a runt (a small pig) in the bag. He would do this to try to cheat the customer. A runt is far less expensive than a full-grown pig. When a customer would ask to see the bag, the farmer would tell the customer he couldn't open the sack because the pig might run away. So if you are buying a pig in a poke, it means you are buying something without seeing it first.

At some point, however, people started to settle. They discovered that the seeds they dropped in the ground grew into plants. They soon understood that food could be grown rather than gathered. It was then that people began to settle in one area. A permanent shelter near water and good soil allowed them to grow their own food. They then began to farm as well as to hunt for food. Soon, small farming communities started to develop.

As people settled into communities, they were able to grow more food than they needed. This meant a farmer could exchange or barter his excess food for tools. Since there were farmers making more food than they needed, others had time to develop skills and crafts that they could exchange for food. As communities grew, it was possible for people to have different jobs. **Archaeologists** (scientists who study ancient sites) have discovered that early civilizations such as the Sumerians had many skilled craftspeople and traders, as well as farmers.

As communities developed, the need for raw materials grew. Raw materials such as wood were needed to construct buildings. Raw materials were not always available where people lived. Many small communities travelled to other communities to trade their goods for raw materials. This, in turn, increased the amount of trading that occurred. Trading was happening within the community, as well as between communities.

The idea of trading goods at a market began thousands of years ago in many parts of the world. The Sumerians were one of the first people to engage in organized trade.

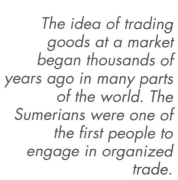

TO MARKET, TO MARKET...

We know some type of organized trade occurred thousands of years ago in the **Middle East**. Archaeologists have found clay tokens dating back 10 000 years. They found them in the ancient city of Ugarit, which was a port in northern Syria. The tokens were probably used as a form of money and were traded for tools, food, or cloth.

Most of the trading was carried out at a market where everyone would bring their goods to sell. People brought food, clothing, and other things to meet their basic needs. They also brought luxury items such as jewellery and pottery.

Markets are still an important means of doing business. What similarities can you see between the ancient Sumerian market and this market in Winnipeg?

SOMETHING TO DO

1. Which items in the list below might be traded at a Sumerian market? Explain your choices.

   hand plough   wooden bucket   pocket watch   vegetables   fruit
   T-shirts   baskets   stone necklaces   pottery   flashlight   cloth   fish
   silk   cinnamon

2. Work in small groups to role-play a scene at a Sumerian market.

   a) Set up a Sumerian market with items that you need in daily life. Make some items more plentiful, some more scarce, and a few rare.

   b) Role-play a bartering session at the market. Use role-play cards such as male, female, child, merchant, etc. Consider add-ons such as wealthy, poor, etc.

   c) Discuss what happened in the bartering session. How successful were the participants? What strategies did and did not work?

3. What types of markets are popular today? What types of goods are sold at these markets? Why do people still enjoy shopping at markets?

3

Sumerians
3000 BCE

1 Sailed to lands bordering the Persian Gulf to obtain ivory and other luxury items. One of the first examples of organized trade.

Babylonians
1300–600 BCE

2 Travelled on foot and rode donkeys and camels. The first known trade agreements were made. Cities that specialized in trade started to spring up.

Phoenecians
1100–700 BCE

3 Used sailing ships to travel along the Aegean Sea. People traded goods, travelled to new areas, and settled there. Empires expanded.

A Brief History of Trade

Crusades
1100–1200 CE

4 Trade declined for 100 years after the fall of the **Roman Empire**. Many luxuries of Asia were once again traded and brought to Europe.

Marco Polo
1270–1295 CE

5 Made a long trip from Europe to the Far East to trade for Chinese goods. There was a demand in Europe for spices and silks.

Great Explorers
1400–1600 CE

6 A period of great exploration. Many trade routes between Europe and Africa, India, and Southeast Asia were established. As sailors set out to trade, they explored unknown lands. Their search for trade routes brought them to North America.

SOMETHING TO DO

1. Work with a partner to role-play a trading scene. Imagine you are an early explorer trying to trade goods, such as spices or gold, with someone who doesn't speak your language. You are trying to negotiate a fair trade, and you need to finds ways to communicate.

   a) What kinds of negotiating and communication strategies would you use?

   b) Discuss how your communication problems might affect trading.

ong before Europeans arrived in Canada, Aboriginal peoples were trading among themselves. Each Aboriginal group was skilled at making certain items. The Algonquian, for example, were excellent canoe builders. They traded with the Huron, who made beautiful fish nets.

When the first explorers came to Canada, they were looking for a trade passage. They wanted to retrieve silks, spices, and gold from Asia. They did not find their passage. Instead they found a harsh and heavily forested land. It didn't take long for them to discover that there was something very valuable here—furs! They knew there was money to be made sending the plentiful Canadian furs back to Europe. The furs were used to make beautiful beaver hats, which were popular among fashionable Europeans. It was the European demand for beaver hats that launched the fur trade.

The Europeans could not have been successful in the fur trading business without the help of Aboriginal peoples. Aboriginal peoples had a knowledge of the waterways, wilderness, travel routes, and trap-

Throughout the 1600s, the French traders established settlements along the St. Lawrence River in the area they called New France. The English traders formed their own colonies in the south along the Atlantic coast, which they called New England. The English were also active in the northern region of Hudson Bay.

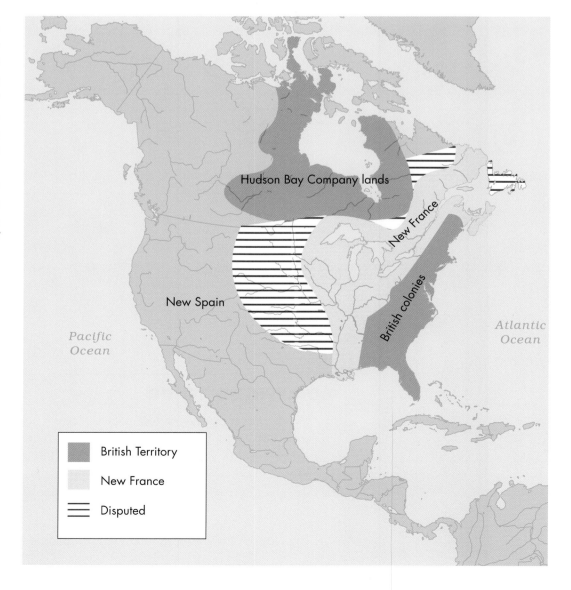

Hudson Bay Company lands

New France

New Spain

British colonies

Pacific Ocean

Atlantic Ocean

British Territory

New France

Disputed

ping techniques. In exchange for their knowledge and furs, the Europeans offered Aboriginal peoples cloth, metal knives, pots, kettles, axes, and guns.

THE HUDSON'S BAY COMPANY

In 1670, a group of English traders founded the Hudson's Bay Company. Their purpose was to build a fur trade network to rival the French traders working out of Montreal. The English traders built a series of small, wooden trading posts around Hudson Bay. The posts, located at the mouths of important rivers, provided easy access to Aboriginal hunters, who often arrived in canoes loaded with furs.

The English had many advantages over the French and were well suited to compete in the trading business. Their posts were close to the fur supplies in the northern forests. They could also transport heavy goods by ships from England to Hudson Bay.

DID YOU KNOW?

Pierre Radisson and his brother-in-law, Medard Grosseilliers, had a plan to visit the "large sea to the north," which Aboriginal peoples said was rich with furs. The French government laughed at their idea, so they went to the English government. A group of English merchants were particularly excited about the two men's ideas. Radisson and Grosseillers quickly became a part of English society, where they were known as "Mr. Radishes and Mr. Gooseberry." The merchants sent the two men back to Canada on a ship called the *Nonsuch*. When the *Nonsuch* returned to England, it was loaded with furs. The delighted merchants promptly applied to the king for a charter and formed a group called the Hudson's Bay Company.

Fur traders were known as voyageurs. They travelled the lakes and rapids in large canoes like this one.

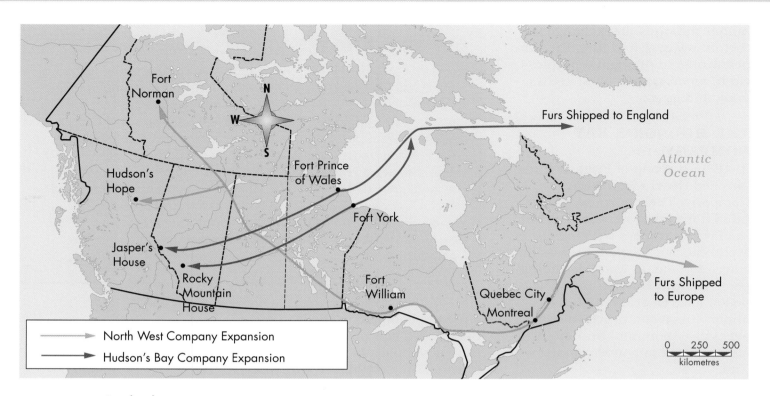

Map legend:
- North West Company Expansion
- Hudson's Bay Company Expansion

As the beaver disappeared from one region after another, traders travelled farther and farther west and north in search of new fur sources.

THE NORTH WEST COMPANY

The English had granted the Hudson's Bay Company the rights to trade furs in all of the lands stretching from Labrador to the Rocky Mountains. The Hudson's Bay Company was not, however, very aggressive when it came to expanding its fur-trading business. The traders were content to have forts only along Hudson Bay and have the fur trappers come to them.

It wasn't long before rival English, French, and American fur traders realized that the Hudson's Bay Company was not actively trapping in Western Canada. With the backing of Montreal merchants, the trappers made their way west of Lake Superior. There they began to build their own fur-trading posts.

In the beginning these fur traders worked alone, competing with each other for furs. But it was expensive to send trappers so far west and the merchants eventually realized they needed to become an organized group of fur traders. They then set up their own company, the

North West Company. The trappers became known as "Nor'Westers." They ventured into new, uncharted areas of Canada. Nor'Westers like Simon Fraser, Alexander MacKenzie, and David Thompson were responsible for exploring and mapping a large portion of western Canada.

For some 40 years, there was bitter and intense competition between the North West and Hudson's Bay companies. Eventually, they realized that the best solution was to combine the two companies. The new company retained the older company's name and became the Hudson's Bay Company.

THE DECLINE OF THE FUR TRADE

For many years, the fur trade continued to be a thriving business. At some point, though, the popular beaver hats were replaced by silk hats, and the fur-trading business declined in North America. During that period, more settlers from Europe came to live in Canada.

They were enticed by the offer of free land and the dream of a new beginning.

At first, clearing the land for farming was difficult and most farmers only cleared enough land to support a family. As land was cleared and farming methods improved, excess crops were produced and sold to other countries. Raw materials and agricultural products, such as timber and corn, soon replaced the fur industry.

MANUFACTURING COMES TO CANADA

During the eighteenth and nineteenth centuries, many business people from across the seas saw Canada as a good place to invest. As money started to come from Europe, small industries started to develop. At the same time, Canadians were starting to sell their manufactured goods on a more frequent basis.

In the twentieth century, the economy experienced another change. From 1900 to 1945 the number of Canadian farmers declined by two-thirds. Canadians were starting to make money from services and manufacturing instead of from agriculture and raw materials.

SOMETHING TO DO

1. Create a photo essay of Canada prior to the 1600s. Cut out pictures from magazines that you think represent what Canada looked like when the first explorers arrived. Select pictures to identify features that would attract explorers to Canada, such as mountains, forests, and lakes. In addition, select pictures to represent items such as metal pots and knives that might have been available at the time for trading. Don't forget to label the pictures.

2. Imagine that you are an early explorer in Canada. Write a letter home describing the new land and your feelings during your first meeting with Aboriginal peoples. Include a sketch of the meeting.

3. Describe the importance of Aboriginal peoples' roles in the early fur trade.

4. What are some reasons for the decline in the fur trade in North America?

5. The Hudson's Bay Company is known today simply as "The Bay." How do you think the company meets the supply and demand of today's customers? Compare the Hudson's Bay Company then and now. You might refer to **http://collections.ic.gc.ca/hbc** to help you in describing the Hudson's Bay Company of the past.

 fun part of collecting trading cards is the excitement that comes with getting a new pack of cards. You're always hoping there's a really valuable card inside. Sometimes, though, you might already have most of the cards in the new package. What, then, do you do with the excess cards — the doubles of those cards that you already have?

motor vehicle parts

What do the goods and services shown on these two pages have in common?

cellphone

lumber

*They are all Canadian **exports**! Goods and services that a country sells to another country are called exports.*

Some people might look at getting a double as an opportunity for a trade. It could be used to trade for something that you need or want. Having more of an item than is necessary, and wanting to sell or exchange it, is what exporting goods is all about.

Exported goods could be raw materials such as wood or minerals such as gold. Other exported goods might include parts made from raw materials such as an engine part made from metals. These exports are sold to manufacturing plants.

The workers at the plant then put them together with other parts to make a **finished product,** such as an automobile. Finally, the finished products are exported.

Countries export both goods and services. We already know that when a person does a job for someone else, they are providing a service. Some examples of services include transportation services related to train and airplane operations and communications services related to the Internet.

DID YOU KNOW?

Bombardier is a large Canadian transportation company. It is an example of a company that sells both goods and services. Bombardier sells goods such as subway trains. It is also paid by other countries to help set up their subway systems. Bombardier is therefore paid for the subway trains, which are the goods, and for the advice and planning, which are the services.

BCE Inc., or Bell Canada Enterprises, is Canada's leading telecommunications company. It includes not only Bell Canada, but many other companies that specialize in communications. The companies provide everything from Internet services such as wireless TV, to telecommunications products such as cellphones.

SOMETHING TO DO

1. In the photos, identify whether each exported good is a raw material, a part, or a finished product.

2. In Did You Know? you learned that companies liked Bombardier and BCE provide services. What other examples of services can you think of?

3. Research a Canadian company that, like Bombardier or BCE, exports both goods and services. Write a brief description of the company, identifying its exports. You might refer to the following site for information: **http://strategis.ic.gc.ca**

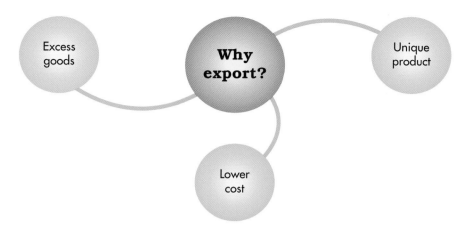

Excess goods

Why export?

Unique product

Lower cost

MAIN REASONS TO EXPORT

A country exports because it is able to produce more of a product than its people need. For example, let's examine one of Canada's exports, timber. Almost half of Canada's land is covered in forests. Canadians cut down trees and sell the timber as a raw material. We also use the timber to produce items such as newsprint. We then sell the paper to other countries. Canada has more timber than its people can use.

A country exports because it is able to produce unique goods and services. Other countries want to buy the items because they are unable to produce the products at home. For example, Canada does not have the climate to grow tropical fruit. Tropical fruits such as oranges grow in warm areas like the southern United States and South America. Therefore the United States exports oranges to countries like Canada.

Coffee beans are another example. There are only certain parts of the world where coffee beans can grow. Countries within Latin America, such as Colombia and Brazil, have the soil and climate that are good for growing coffee beans. Other countries buy these coffee beans because they can't grow the beans themselves.

A country exports because it is able to produce goods at a low cost. When producing goods, there are lots of costs involved. One example is **labour costs**, or what a company pays its workers. If wages are low, it will cost less to make the goods. A country will be successful in exporting the goods to other countries because the final cost will be lower.

Canada uses timber to produce export items such as furniture and cellophane.

CANADIAN EXPORTS

Many years ago, some of Canada's main exports were wheat, copper, timber, and wood pulp. Canada remains one of the largest exporters of forestry products. We still sell timber, as well as the many products made from timber.

Agricultural products such as wheat, barley, oats, corn, livestock, and red meat are still an important part of Canada's exports. Our leading export in this area is wheat. Our wheat fields are bigger than some European countries!

Canada's exports have, however, changed over time. We still sell our forestry and agricultural products, but we now export more automotive parts, machinery, and equipment.

Canadian exports are also expanding to include information technology, communications equipment, computer software and services, and chemicals used to make products such as shampoo, toothpaste, and soap.

In the past 10 years, Canadian companies have worked hard to stay on the leading edge of communication and information technology. Canadian telephone companies have successfully experimented with fibre optics, which advances our ability to send information from person to person. Canadian technology has also been responsible for the development of many satellites, which send information quickly from place to place. This high-tech trend will undoubtedly continue. More and more Canadian companies will develop faster and more efficient ways to communicate with people around the world.

Canada has a highly educated and skilled **work force**. In other words, our work force, or the total number of Canadians able to work, has lots of expertise to offer the world. Most of Canada's exported services are in the travel industry, the government, nuclear technology, financial services, and telecommunications.

Canadian exports, 2000

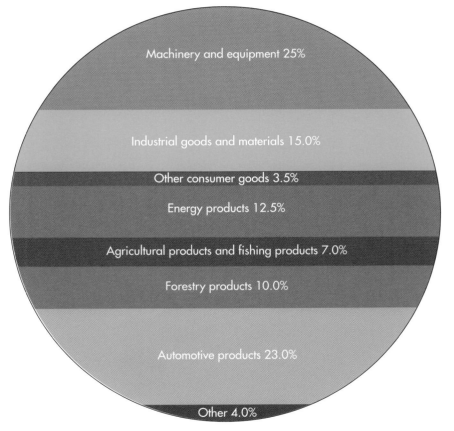

Machinery and equipment 25%

Industrial goods and materials 15.0%

Other consumer goods 3.5%

Energy products 12.5%

Agricultural products and fishing products 7.0%

Forestry products 10.0%

Automotive products 23.0%

Other 4.0%

Source: Adapted from www.statcan.ca

SOMETHING TO DO

1. Refer to the export categories in the pie graph. List each of the following items under the appropriate export category.

   flour   lobsters   newsprint   gasoline   furniture   copper   wheat
   subway system expertise   lumber   nickel   farm tractors   nuclear expertise
   space technology expertise   aircraft machinery   vans   natural gas
   car parts   clothing

NATURAL RESOURCES

Canada has always been known as a country rich in **natural resources**. Natural resources are the parts of the environment that are useful to people, such as timber, oil, natural gas, minerals, farmland, and water. We export our natural resources to countries all over the world.

Some of our resources are **renewable**. In other words, they can be replaced once we have used them. We can plant new trees and new fish can be born. Unfortunately, when we use up these renewable resources too quickly, nature is not able to keep up with the pace. Then it may take many years before the resource increases to an acceptable level.

Examine this map to discover some of the resources Canada has to offer the world.

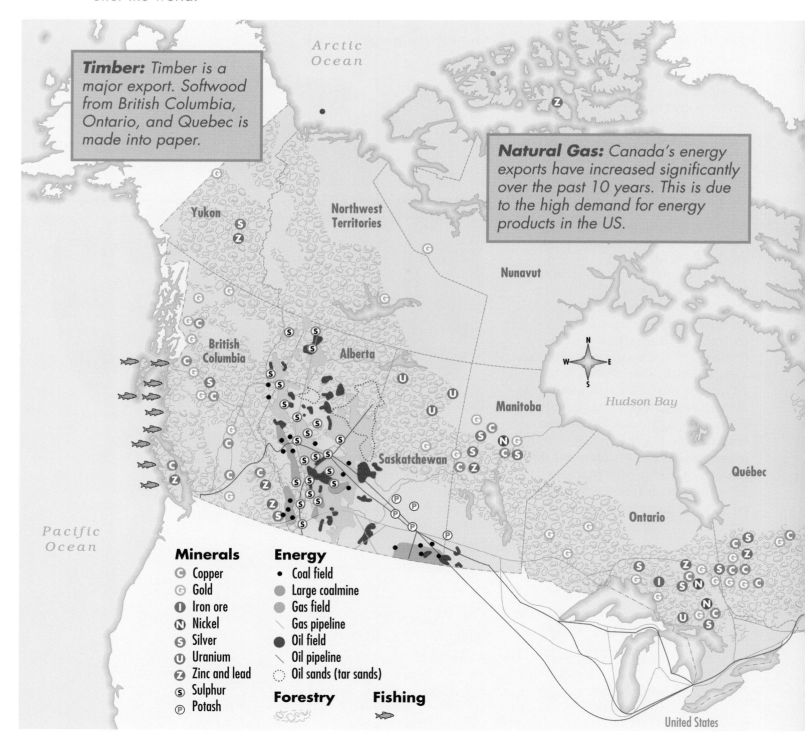

Timber: Timber is a major export. Softwood from British Columbia, Ontario, and Quebec is made into paper.

Natural Gas: Canada's energy exports have increased significantly over the past 10 years. This is due to the high demand for energy products in the US.

Arctic Ocean

Yukon

Northwest Territories

Nunavut

British Columbia

Alberta

Manitoba

Hudson Bay

Saskatchewan

Québec

Ontario

Pacific Ocean

United States

Minerals
- **C** Copper
- **G** Gold
- **I** Iron ore
- **N** Nickel
- **S** Silver
- **U** Uranium
- **Z** Zinc and lead
- **S** Sulphur
- **P** Potash

Energy
- • Coal field
- Large coalmine
- Gas field
- \ Gas pipeline
- Oil field
- \ Oil pipeline
- Oil sands (tar sands)

Forestry

Fishing

What Is an Export?

Resources that are **non-renewable** are those that, once used, will never come back again or may take millions of years to come back. Oil, natural gas, and minerals such as copper are examples of resources that are non-renewable.

FRESH WATER

Fresh water is one of Canada's most abundant renewable resources. Therefore many of us tend to take this resource for granted. Perhaps this is why Canadians are the second largest users of water in the world.

Average Daily Water Consumption (at home, per person)	
United States	500 L
Canada	340 L
United Kingdom	200 L
France	150 L
Israel	135 L
Madagascar	6 L
Source: Environment Canada	

If you had only 6 litres of water a day, what would you use it for?

Greenland

Water: *We have more fresh water than any other country in the world. The government is thinking about whether we should export our water in the future.*

Mining: *Canada has many mineral resources, including copper, zinc, iron ore, gold, lead, and nickel. Canada is one of the world's largest exporters of minerals.*

Fishing: *Fish stocks have dropped drastically in the past 10 years due to overfishing. Now the fishing catch is restricted until stocks build back up again.*

Newfoundland and Labrador

Prince Edward Island

New Brunswick

Nova Scotia

Atlantic Ocean

0   300   600
kilometres

SOMETHING TO DO

1. Use the chart to estimate how much water you use and how much water your family uses in a day. Suggest ways to decrease the amount of water you use.

Water Consumption	
washing clothes	150 L
having a bath	120 L
having a shower	75 L
dishwasher (per load)	45 L
leaky tap (per day)	25 L
flushing the toilet	20 L
brushing teeth	6 L

o you recall Lee and his connections to the world? Have a look at the labels on your shirt and shoes. Think about the juice you drank this morning or the fruit you ate at lunch. Most likely, much of what you wear, eat, and drink is not made in Canada. These things are made in other countries, bought by companies in Canada, then sold to you, your parents, or your school. These products are imported!

What do all these goods and services have in common? SUV

*They are all Canadian **imports**! Goods and services that a country buys from another country are called imports.*

transportation services

petroleum

MAIN REASONS TO IMPORT

If a country imports, it doesn't mean that its people can't produce the goods or services. Most imports are similar to those produced within the country, but are different in quality or price. Although Canada produces many goods and services, there are countries that can produce a better or cheaper version. The imported goods or services may also have different features than those produced in Canada. Canadians prefer to have a choice when they shop, so we import many items from all over the world. Importing makes it possible to purchase a greater variety of goods and services.

A country also imports when it cannot produce goods and services domestically. For example, a country may not have the right climate to grow certain crops or the raw materials to make certain goods, so it imports. **Developing countries** rely heavily on imports because they produce little food and have few manufacturing plants. Therefore they have to import these items from developed countries. Developed countries are countries like Canada in which most people

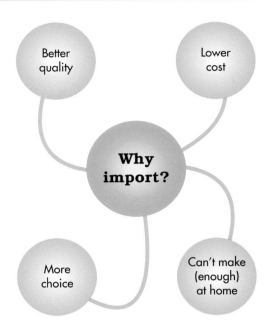

Why import?
- Better quality
- Lower cost
- More choice
- Can't make (enough) at home

have adequate food and housing and can afford some luxury items. People in developing countries may face food shortages and poor housing and cannot afford luxury items.

Even developed countries such as Japan rely heavily on countries like Canada for some products. Japan is very mountainous, with little room for farms. Therefore farmers can harvest only 50 per cent of the food needed to feed all of the people in the country. Since Japan is not able to produce enough food on its own, it has to import many agricultural products from other countries.

Japan also relies on other countries for raw materials. It imports such items as iron ore, copper, and aluminum to make computers, watches, and many other products. Japan then exports the finished products to other countries. Japan would not have such a strong economy today if it did not import.

IMPORT TO EXPORT? CRAZY TRADING!

Colombia is known for exporting some of the highest quality coffee beans in the world. During the late 1990s, however, heavy rains in Colombia resulted in a poor coffee bean crop. The bean plants did not produce enough quality beans. As a result, Colombia could not fill all of its international orders.

Colombia did not want to damage its reputation and lose customers. So it decided to import quality coffee beans from other countries. The imported beans were in turn used to fill all of Colombia's orders. As you can imagine, little profit was made this way. But Colombia was willing to import beans, then turn around and export them to satisfy its customers. They hoped the following year would bring a better growing season.

SOMETHING TO DO

1. How many imports can you find in your home? List them under various categories, such as clothing, electronics, games, and food. Beside each item identify the country of origin. Draw conclusions about the origins of most of our imports. Consider, for example, from what country the majority of the items are from and why.

2. Next time you go to the store see if you can find two similar items, for example, two shirts, one made in Canada and one made in another country. Find some similarities and differences between the products. Compare the price and quality. Which product would you buy?

CANADIAN IMPORTS

What do you think Canada imports the most? Would you say it is food, clothing, or perhaps electronics?

Our chief import is machinery and equipment! Eighty-five per cent of our imports are parts and finished products such as machinery, motor vehicle products, industrial and electronic goods, computers, and consumer goods. Machinery might include a tractor for a farmer or a piece of equipment for a factory. Electronic goods might include televisions or electronic games. Motor vehicle parts are those used in factories to build cars, trucks, and vans. Other major imports include processed foods, beverages, crude petroleum, and chemicals.

Canada also imports services. We import more services than we export. Travel and transportation services are imported the most.

We also import many business services. We pay experts from other countries to provide us with research and development services, insurance, and transportation services.

Buying Imports

During the warmer months in Ontario, we grow and sell many agricultural products. During that time, we also import many of the same crops and sell the products in our stores. Sometimes the produce from other countries can actually cost less than those items grown here.

One of the reasons is labour costs. The labour costs may be lower in the country from which we imported the goods. Bringing in cheaper fruits and vegetables that compete with Canadian-grown crops presents a problem for Canadian farmers. Canadian farmers have a hard time making money if we buy imported crops rather than Canadian crops.

Canadian imports, 2000

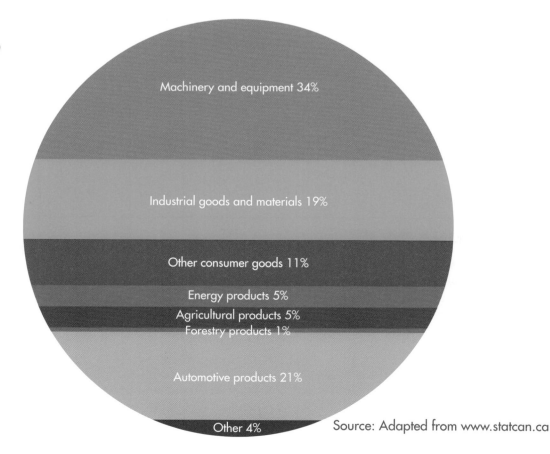

Machinery and equipment 34%

Industrial goods and materials 19%

Other consumer goods 11%

Energy products 5%

Agricultural products 5%

Forestry products 1%

Automotive products 21%

Other 4%

Source: Adapted from www.statcan.ca

Buy Canadian!

SOMETHING TO DO

1. Refer to the import categories in the pie graph. List each of the following items under the appropriate import category.

   clothing   cameras   computers   iron ore   oranges   steel   petroleum
   teak wood   airplanes   peanuts   toothpaste   grapefruit   tomato
   potatoes   soap   plastic containers   cars   shoes   banking services

2. Select one import or export. Using the Statistics Canada Web site at **www.statcan.ca** find the total value of sales for the past five years. Record your findings on a line graph. What does your graph tell you about the sale of that export in the past five years? Using the graph, predict what the sales of the export will be in the next year, in two years, and in five years.

DID YOU KNOW?

Do you go out of your way to buy Canadian products? Do you ever look at the label to see if a product is made in Canada? Some people feel strongly that we should buy the products made in our own country. When we buy goods made at home, we are helping to make sure Canadians have jobs. We are, in fact, supporting our own country's economy.

When two countries exchange imports and exports, they are **trading partners**. Canada is one of the 10 largest trading partners in the world. We trade with more than 40 countries. Canada has one of the richest economies in the world. Trading with many nations is very important to Canada's economy. Twenty per cent of Canadian jobs rely on trade. In other words, 20 out of every 100 people have jobs that are somehow related to trade.

The United States is our largest trading partner. We send over 85 per cent of our exports to the United States. In return, the US supplies Canada with almost 70 per cent of our imports. Canada trades with the United States more than with all other countries combined. In Canada, 2 million people have jobs because of the amount that we export to the United States. A similar culture, close proximity, and a common language make it easy for trade to occur.

Much of the trading happens between the United States and Ontario. Americans trade more with just the province of Ontario than they do with Japan!

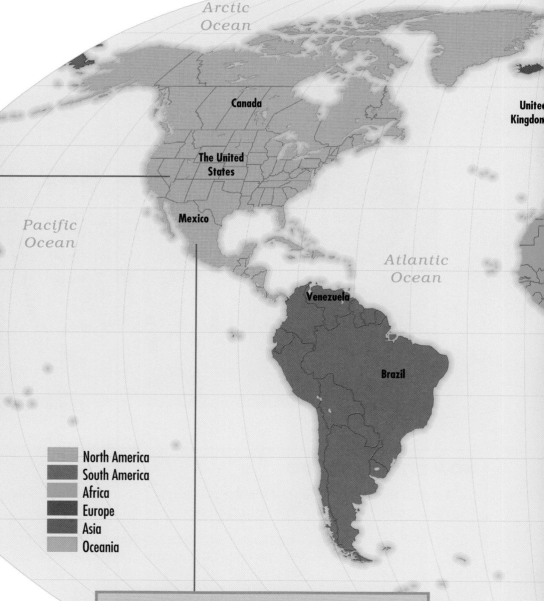

North America
South America
Africa
Europe
Asia
Oceania

Mexico is an important trading partner. Canada imports five times more products than it exports to Mexico. Inexpensive labour is one reason why Canada imports large quantities from Mexico.

Canada's Trading Partners

Britain is one of Canada's oldest trading partners. Today, Britain sells products such as aircraft parts, medical instruments, crude oil, machinery, cars, and car parts.

Japan is Canada's second largest trading partner, accounting for approximately 5 per cent of Canada's imports and 2 per cent of our exports. In 2000, Japan sold almost $11 billion worth of products to Canada. Canada sold approximately $9 billion worth of products to Japan.

DID YOU KNOW?

We export over a third of what we produce. In 2000, Canada exported approximately $410 billion worth of goods and services. We imported slightly more goods and services than we exported.

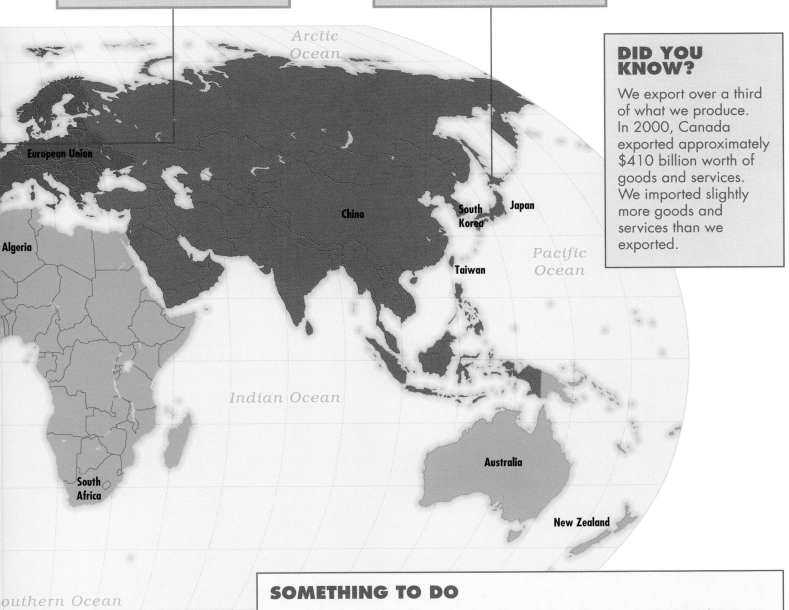

Arctic Ocean

European Union

Algeria

China

South Korea

Japan

Taiwan

Pacific Ocean

Indian Ocean

South Africa

Australia

New Zealand

Southern Ocean

SOMETHING TO DO

1. Name some jobs that are related to and are dependent upon trade. How and why are they related to trade?

2. Create a "picture-passport" for someone who is travelling around the world. After you read about each country in this chapter, select a picture from a magazine to represent that country. On each page of the passport, write the name of the country beside the picture.

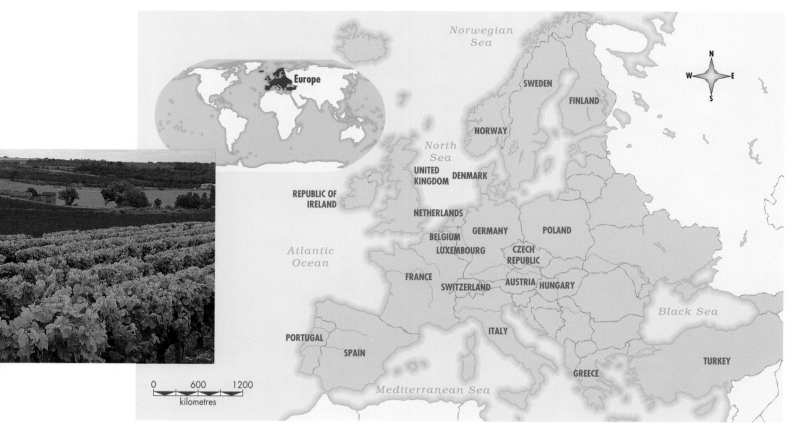

In southern France, vineyards and lavender fields cover the landscape. What are some of the agricultural products grown in your region or province?

EUROPE

Europe is the second smallest continent in the world, but it has the second largest population.

Europe has historically been known for its great explorations. Many places worldwide have been influenced by this exploration. As a result, Spanish, French, and English are spoken all over the world.

Today, most countries that were once **colonies** of European countries now govern themselves. Canada is one of those countries. We are still governed by English law and have both French and English as our official languages.

Warm summers, cool winters, and plenty of rain make Europe ideal for farming. Europe has the greatest percentage of farmland of all the continents.

Much of Europe's wealth comes from factories and mines. Northern France, Belgium, and Germany are major manufacturing centres. They depend upon their natural resources, including iron ore, coal, oil, and natural gas, to manufacture goods. Most of the countries are surrounded by water, leaving many available harbours for shipping the goods. Machinery, motor vehicles, iron and steel, and plastic products all come from Germany. Italy is also an important trading partner with Canada.

Many of the countries in Europe and the United Kingdom are joined together in an organization called the **European Union**. For many years each country had its own **currency**, or money. A new form of money, the Euro, is now used in many European countries. It allows for easier trading and business transactions.

DID YOU KNOW?

There are many advantages for the countries that belong to the European Union. They form a stronger trading block when dealing with other countries. They give each other a "cut" on taxes for goods and services traded within the EU. They have the power to attract global contracts for finished products by assigning parts out to individual countries in their group.

ASIA

Asia is the largest continent in the world, covering nearly one-third of the world's total land area. It is larger than North and South America combined. Asia also has the largest population of any continent. Six out of every 10 people in the world live in Asia.

Rice is the main source of food for the people on this continent. Crop failures, poor farming methods, and war have forced many countries in Asia to import food from the United States and Canada.

The region known as the Middle East is also part of Asia. It includes Egypt, Sudan, Israel, Lebanon, Iran, Iraq, Kuwait, Jordan, Bahrain, Syria, Saudi Arabia, and Turkey.

The most important natural resource in the Middle East is oil. Vast oil reserves are found around the Persian Gulf. Countries around the world, including Canada, import much of their oil from this region. This has made oil-producing countries such as Saudi Arabia, Kuwait, and Bahrain very wealthy. In turn, they have become good markets for manufactured goods from other countries.

Many countries in Asia are important trading partners for Canada. In addition to Japan, China is an important Asian trading partner. China places in the top five

Rice is an important food source in many parts of Asia. These Chinese farmers are working in terraced rice fields.

Asia

when we look at the countries from which Canada imports. Some of the more unique products imported from China are toys and games, sports equipment, and clothing. South Korea and Taiwan are two other important trading partners. Their products include clothing, electronic and electrical equipment, cars, ships, textiles, and plywood.

SOUTH AMERICA

The Amazon River and the Andes Mountains are commonly associated with South America. It is a continent of rugged and beautiful terrain and highly populated cities. The Amazon rain forest, found in South America, is the largest in the world. It holds some of the world's most exotic creatures, such as

Rio de Janeiro is one of Latin America's most exciting cities. Much of the action centres along Copacabana Beach, shown here.

South America

parrots and monkeys. Today, much of this forest is being stripped away for roads, mining, farmland, and cities.

Most of South America's population lives in large cities along the coastline. Cities such as Rio de Janeiro, Buenos Aires, Santiago, Lima, and Caracas are bursting at the seams with people.

The continent's largest country is Brazil. It is also Canada's biggest South American trading partner. Coffee, fruit and vegetable juice, and footwear are some of the products Canada imports from Brazil. Venezuela is Canada's second largest South American trading partner. Tobacco and footwear are two of the products we import from there.

AFRICA

Africa is the second largest continent — and the warmest! It is a land full of contrasting landforms. Here you'll find huge plains (flat stretches of land) and tropical grasslands that are home to herds of animals. The desert

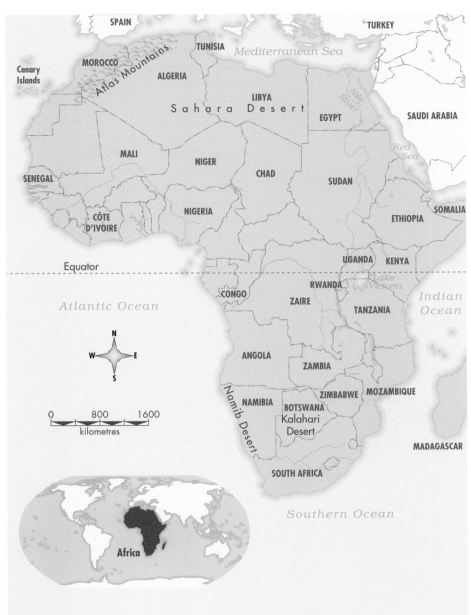

Africa

When you think of Africa, you probably imagine jungles and wild animals. But if you were to visit Africa today, you would see many urban areas with skyscrapers such as in Nairobi, Kenya.

supports few animals and plants. Main desert regions include the Sahara in the north and the Kalahari and Namib in the south. There are also large mountain ranges and a tropical rain forest around the Equator. Fifty per cent of Africa's natural rain forests have been cleared for timber and farming.

There are 52 independent countries in Africa. Algeria and South Africa are Canada's two biggest African trading partners. Algeria ships petroleum products to Canada, while South Africa sells fruits, nuts, and precious metals such as diamonds and gold.

Africa has precious resources such as copper, diamonds, gold, and oil. Diamond mining is an important source of income in several African countries. Future economic growth in Africa may depend on the development of its oil and gas reserves. Canada has expertise in the area of oil and gas exploration and production. It could sell this expertise as a service to Africa.

OCEANIA

Oceania derives its name from the Pacific Ocean. This region includes Australia, New Zealand, and the many small island countries of the South Pacific.

Australia is by far the largest country in Oceania. It is the sixth largest country in the world. Australia is a land of forests, deserts, and scrub. It has animals and birds, such as the kangaroo and kookaburra, that are not found anywhere else in the world.

Eastern Australia's soil is ideal for growing crops and raising sheep

Oceania

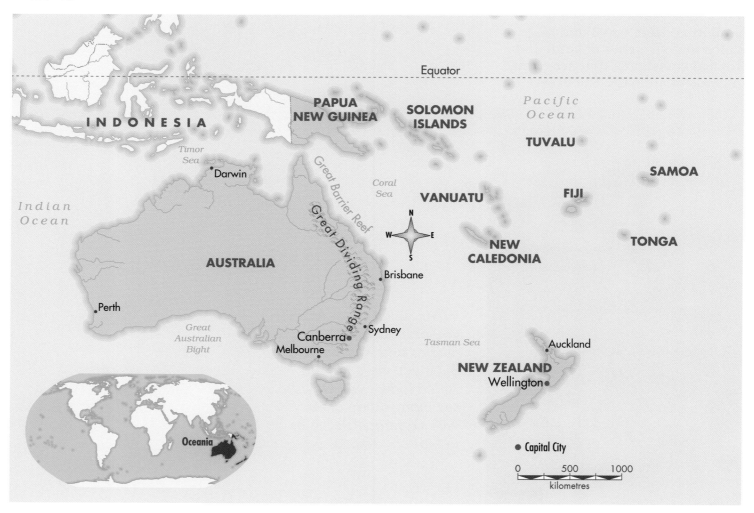

and cattle. Most of Australia's largest cities are situated in this area. Raw sugar, beef, wine, and nickel are a few examples of goods exported today from Australia.

Lamb is a major export for New Zealand. Sheep even outnumber the people on this island country! There are 20 sheep for every person living in New Zealand.

These laughing kookaburras are among the unique wildlife found in Australia.

SOMETHING TO DO

1. Work with a partner to make an outline that shows the topics, subtopics, and main ideas discussed in this chapter. What other formats would you use to present the material?

2. Work in groups of six to present information on one country in this chapter.

   a) Have each member of your group select one country from each region: Europe; Latin America; Asia; Africa; Oceania.

   b Using an almanac, discover the main exports of that country. Create symbols to represent these exports.

   c) Label the following on an outline map of the country: a title, major cities, major waterways, a legend identifying the export symbols.

3. Use an atlas to help you answer the following questions:

   a) Does your family have a link to another country? If so, in what continent can the country be found? Did your ancestors come from another country? If so, what part of the world?

   b) Do some research to discover what the country is best known for. Find out about its exports and unique products.

ave you ever set up a row of dominoes on their ends one behind the other? What happened when you pushed the first domino? Did they all tumble one right after the other? Isn't it fascinating to watch the effects of the dominoes toppling upon each other?

In many ways today's world functions like a row of dominoes. What happens in one country often affects neighbouring countries, and even countries far across the world.

The Economy

Importing and exporting goods and services provide jobs. Jobs put money into the hands of Canadian consumers. Canadians enjoy one of the highest standards of living in the world. This means that most Canadians have a job, own or rent a home, and have enough food to eat and extra money to spend on entertainment and some luxury items.

Immigration

People in other countries get to know some things about Canada through trade. Sometimes this results in people wanting to move to Canada. When people from other countries come to Canada they bring their cultures, religions, and values with them. Canada respects and encourages these differences.

Foreign Aid

Canada is an active participant in peacekeeping missions. As a result, much of the world has a positive view of Canadians. Canada's role in the global community also includes helping developing countries. Through governments and private charities, money, services, technology, and goods are sent to other countries as **foreign aid**.

Global Connections

Global Disturbances

There are many advantages to the global economy, but there are problems as well. The links that connect us also mean that a negative development in one country can result in a negative effect in another country.

Foreign Investment

Many foreign companies invest money in Canada in land, buildings, manufacturing plants, and service businesses. Our skilled work force, stable economy, and technological know-how make Canada a good place for **foreign investment**. Foreign investment creates jobs for Canadians and helps to keep the economy strong.

HOW DOES TRADE CONNECT US TO THE WORLD?

New Technology

The Internet allows Canadians to be in touch with people around the world in seconds. It even makes communication with people in remote areas of the world possible. Canadians can trade **on-line** without ever meeting the person with whom they are trading.

Variety Is the Spice of Life

When Canadians shop, they have access to many foreign products. Food, clothing, furniture, appliances—even music and films—are imported from all over the world.

SOMETHING TO DO

1. Design a poster that would attract immigrants to Canada.

2. If you have a friend or relative in another country, send an e-mail or write a letter to him or her explaining why Canada is a great place to live.

**ime zones** are always an important and practical issue when trading. You can call, fax, or e-mail your customer, but what happens if nobody is there to answer? Imagine the problem for an exporter in Toronto, Canada, who wants to communicate with a customer in Tokyo, Japan. It is noon in Toronto, but in Tokyo it is 2 a.m. Everyone is in bed. This would definitely not be a good time to do business!

What exactly are time zones? How do they affect our daily lives?

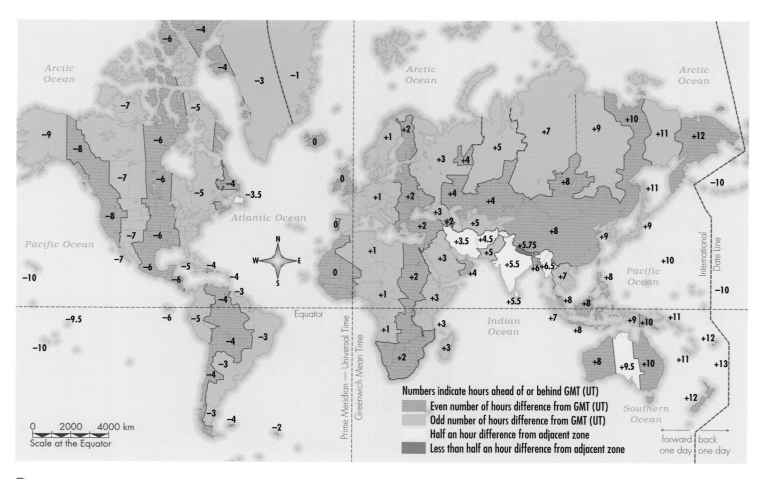

Time zones

STANDARDIZING THE WORLD

The world is always spinning on its axis. It takes 24 hours to complete one rotation. As the sun begins to rise in Canada, on the opposite side of the world the sun is setting. In other words, it is the middle of the night and dark in Australia when it is 1:00 in the afternoon in Ontario!

The world is so large that it has been divided into 24 different time zones, one for each hour of the clock. Because the world's **circumference**, or the distance around the circle, is 360°, each time zone is approximately 15° of longitude (360 ÷ 24 = 15). Longitudinal lines are imaginary lines running from the North to South poles around the world, at equal distances apart. Thus, time changes one hour for every 15° of longitude. Sometimes the lines separating a time zone are altered to take into account political borders or natural boundaries.

Prime Meridian

The longitudinal line that passes through Greenwich in London, England, is numbered 0° and is called the **Prime Meridian**. Time is counted from this line. Moving east, time is calculated as plus (+) **Greenwich Mean Time.** Moving west, time is calculated as minus (−) Greenwich Mean Time. So, travellers heading east need to set their watches ahead one hour for every time zone they pass through. West-bound, they need to set their watches back.

International Date Line

The **International Date Line** is a place where one day ends and the other begins. This imaginary line is at 180° longitude. The time is the same on both sides of the Date Line, but if you travel from east to west you move ahead one full day. If you travel from west to east you go back one day. For example, if you were flying from Canada across the Pacific Ocean to Russia (east to west), you would cross the International Date Line and it would be one day later.

Time zones are an important factor when trading. Business people trying to reach people in other countries need to be aware of the time. They need to be sure that the person they are calling will actually be in the office!

It is also important to consider the difference in time when travelling long distances. Flying from one country to the other will result in passing through many time zones.

Adjusting to another country's time zone can be difficult for travellers. For example, if you left Vancouver at 9:00 a.m. and arrived in Toronto four hours later, it would be 1:00 p.m. in Vancouver. You would be ready for lunch. However, you would have passed through three time zones, and in Toronto it would be 4:00 p.m. People would have eaten lunch long ago. Now they'd be starting to think about dinner!

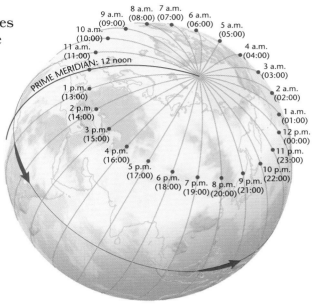

Across Canada, there are six standard time zones.

SOMETHING TO DO

1. Look at the time zones map. Find the largest country to have just one time zone.

2. How many time zones are there between Halifax, Nova Scotia, and Vancouver, British Columbia? If it is 6:00 p.m. in Halifax, what time is it in Vancouver?

3. How many time zones are there between Toronto and Germany? If you are travelling from Toronto to Germany, will you lose time or gain time? If it is 3:00 p.m. in Toronto, what time is it in Germany?

4. How many time zones are there between Toronto, Ontario, and Johannesburg, South Africa? If it is 2:00 a.m. in Toronto, what time is it in Johannesburg?

he United States is so vast that it has every type of climate, from continental (very cold winters and warmer summers) to coastal (mild winters and warm summers), subtropical (warm winters and hot summers) to high mountain (cold winters and cool summers). On the same day it can be cold, snowy, and icy in the northern states and very hot in the southern states.

Landforms

Two mountain ranges run through the United States. In the west lie the Rocky Mountains. They run from Alaska south through British Columbia and the American states of Montana and Wyoming before ending in Colorado. The Appalachians are on the eastern side of the country. Beginning in the Canadian province of New Brunswick, they head south through many eastern states, including Pennsylvania, Tennessee, and Kentucky, until they reach Alabama.

Between the two mountain ranges are the Great Plains. Plains are large, flat stretches of land. The mighty Mississippi River winds its way through these plains. The Mississippi is the largest river in North America.

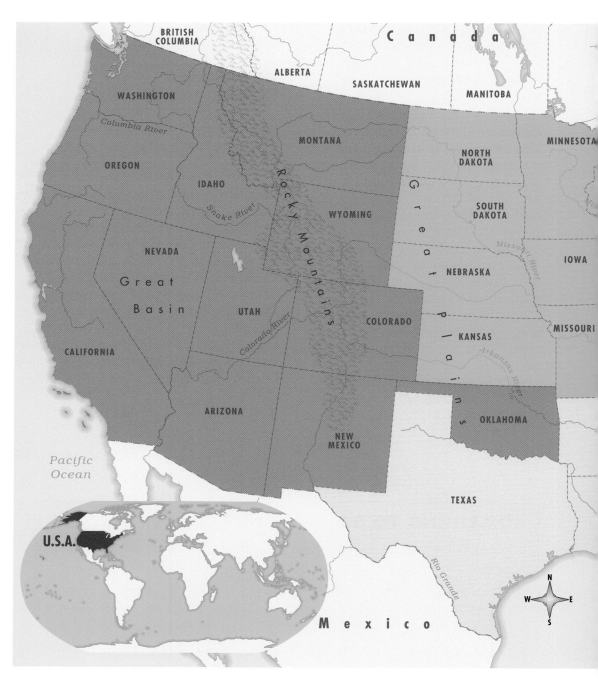

The United States contains many different regions with a variety of climates and landscapes. In this chapter, we'll look at the four main regions: the Northeastern, Midwestern, Southern, and Western regions. Locate these regions on the map.

Facts

- The United States is the fourth largest country in the world, covering more than 9 372 610 square kilometres. It stretches from the Pacific Ocean to the Atlantic Ocean.
- There are 50 states, as well as the District of Columbia. Each state has its own capital. Washington, the capital of the United States, is located in the District of Columbia.
- There are 48 states that lie between Mexico and Canada. The remaining two states, Hawaii and Alaska, are located away from the mainland.
- More than 275 million people live in the United States.

Northeast Region
Midwestern Region
Southern Region
Western Region

The White House, located in Washington D.C., is the home of the President of the United States. A president is elected to office every four years.

SOMETHING TO DO

1. Survey your class to find out how many students have visited the United States. Find out where they have visited and why.

2. As you are reading this chapter, select two regions that you have visited or would like to visit. Create a Venn diagram and compare the two regions in terms of *two* of the following: landforms, climate, industry, agriculture, and tourism.

NORTHEASTERN REGION

Raging rivers and beautiful lakes dominate this part of the United States. The northern part of the region is often referred to as New England while the southern is called the Mid-Atlantic states. Many of the states lie along the Atlantic Ocean.

To the north lies Lake Ontario and Lake Erie. The lakes form part of the border between the United States and Canada. Many of the states, such as Maine, Vermont, New Hampshire, and New York, border Canada. The magnificent Appalachian Mountains lie farther inland.

Large numbers of people live in some of the big cities within this region. Thriving cities include Boston, Philadelphia, Baltimore, Washington, and New York.

Industry Facts

- This region is the manufacturing hub of the US. Everything from clocks, bicycles, cigars, and combs have at one time been manufactured here.
- Electronics (cameras) and communications equipment (telephones) are manufactured in this region today.
- Maine is an important boot and shoe manufacturer and one of the world's largest pulp-paper producers. Connecticut factories produce everything from weapons and sewing machines to cutlery and clocks.
- This region is known for coal mining and steel production.
- Highways, railways, and airports allow goods to be transported quickly and easily. The harbours along the Atlantic coast enable ships to carry products around the world.
- Many powerful rivers provide opportunities to produce hydroelectric power.

The Northeastern Region includes Connecticut, Maine, Massachusetts, New Hampshire, Rhode Island, Vermont, New Jersey, New York, Pennsylvania, and the District of Columbia.

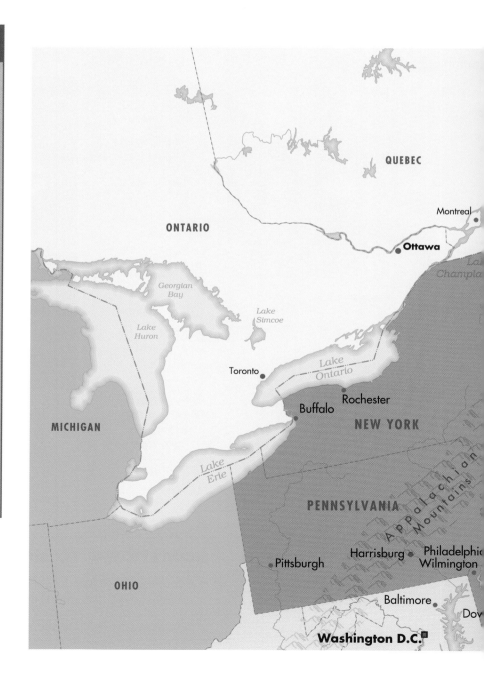

New York City is the largest city in the United States. With a population of over 7 million, it has more people than most Canadian provinces.

Tourism Facts

- Maine is a popular vacation spot because of the quiet little fishing harbours and picturesque villages.
- The ski resorts in Vermont, New York, and New Hampshire are widely popular.

Agriculture Facts

- Vermont is best known for its maple syrup. It ranks second to the world's top producers, Ontario and Quebec.
- Massachusetts is the nation's leading cranberry producer. Maine is a leading producer of blueberries. Each state grows a variety of fruits and vegetables.
- Cattle and chickens are important farm products. Dairy products such as milk and cheese are sold to many markets.
- Many people living in the villages along the coast make their living by fishing. Sardines and lobsters are two of the catches.

SOMETHING TO DO

1. Create a map of the Northeastern Region. Identify major cities. Create symbols to represent industry, agriculture, and tourism features associated with the region. Place the symbols on the map and create a legend to identify what they represent.

2. Design four or five symbols to represent the Northeastern Region. Create a flag for the region using these symbols.

MIDWESTERN REGION

Between the Rocky Mountains and the Appalachian Mountains lies a flat, fertile land known as the Great Plains. This area is often referred to as the farm belt because it contains some of the world's finest farmland.

To the north of Ohio and Michigan lie three of the Great Lakes: Lakes Erie, Michigan, and Superior. Each of these lakes, except Lake Michigan, is shared with Canada. Lake Michigan lies completely within the US.

The Great Plains share many characteristics with the Prairies of central Canada. In both countries, this flat land is used mainly for growing wheat and grazing cattle. In both Canada and the United States, this region is also known for its cold winters!

The Midwestern Region includes Illinois, Indiana, Iowa, Kansas, Michigan, Minnesota, Missouri, Nebraska, North Dakota, Ohio, South Dakota, and Wisconsin.

Industry Facts

- Ohio is a diverse manufacturing state. Each of its main cities is known for a different type of manufacturing: for example, Akron for rubber, Cincinnati for jet engines and machine tools, and Cleveland for auto assembly.
- Some of the larger cities around the Great Lakes, such as Cleveland, Detroit, and Chicago, are busy manufacturing centres.
- For many years, Detroit, known as the Motor City, manufactured more cars than any other city in the world.
- The Midwest has access to railways, harbours, airports, and highways. The Great Lakes and the Mississippi River provide fast water routes for ships exporting iron ore and wheat.
- Many states are rich in natural resources, such as coal, salt, iron, copper, and limestone. Minnesota produces 75 per cent of the country's iron ore.
- Missouri's economy relies on the service industry to provide many jobs, such as working in restaurants and hotels and driving taxis.

ONTARIO

● Capital City

WISCONSIN

MICHIGAN

Milwaukee
Madison
Lansing ● Detroit
Ann Arbor

Chicago

Cleveland

ILLINOIS   INDIANA   OHIO

Columbus

Springfield   Indianapolis   ● Dayton
Cincinnati

St. Louis   Louisville

Ohio River   KENTUCKY

Lake Superior
Lake Michigan
Lake Huron
Lake Erie

0 100 200 300 400
kilometres

Agriculture Facts

- The large stretches of flat, fertile land allow most of the United States' wheat and corn to be grown here. The region grows one half of the world's corn. Iowa and Nebraska are centres for wheat and corn production.
- Hot days, warm nights, and the right amount of rainfall make the region ideal for growing other grains. In addition to wheat, farmers grow alfalfa, barley, oats, and rye. Iowa and Illinois are leading soybean-producing states.
- Apples, cherries, beans, pears, grapes, potatoes, and sugar beats are harvested in Michigan. Similar vegetables and fruits are grown in other states of the region.
- Farm animals are an important part of this area's economy. Wisconsin is America's dairyland. Both milk and milk products, such as cheese, are sold to markets. Illinois and Iowa are major hog producers.

Wheat farming is an important agricultural activity in the Midwestern Region. It takes a large crew and lots of equipment to harvest the crop. This farm is in Kansas.

Tourism Facts

- Mark Twain's boyhood home in Missouri helps lure tourists to this state.
- Mount Rushmore, where the faces of past presidents Thomas Jefferson, Abraham Lincoln, George Washington, and Theodore Roosevelt are carved into the mountain, can be found in South Dakota.
- Tourists enjoy visiting Dodge City, Kansas. This city is like a page out of an old western movie.

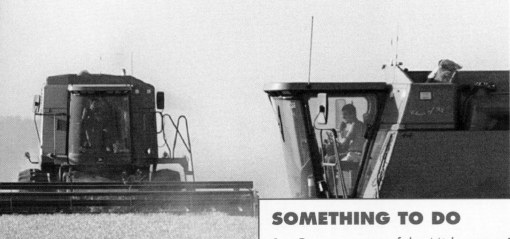

SOMETHING TO DO

1. Create a map of the Midwestern Region, similar to the one you did for the Northeastern Region. Identify major cities. Create symbols to represent industry, agriculture, and tourism features associated with the region. Place the symbols on the map and create a legend to identify what each symbol represents.

2. Compare the Prairies in Canada and the Midwestern Region of the United States in terms of landforms and climate.

SOUTHERN REGION

This region extends from the Atlantic Coast in the east to the Mexican border in the west. The Mississippi River runs through the centre of the region and empties into the Gulf of Mexico. To the south, you will find the Gulf of Mexico; to the east, the Atlantic Ocean. Inland, the Appalachian Mountains run through several of the southern states.

Florida, well-known to many Canadians, extends farther south than any other state. Most of the southern states have a mild climate. Even in a more northern state, such as Georgia, the average January temperature is 10°C.

Hurricanes are known to strike in the southern states along the Atlantic and Gulf of Mexico coasts in late summer and early fall.

The Southern Region includes Alabama, Arkansas, Delaware, Florida, Georgia, Kentucky, Louisiana, Maryland, Mississippi, North Carolina, South Carolina, Tennessee, Texas, Virginia, and West Virginia.

Industry Facts

- Once known primarily for growing tobacco and cotton, the South has recently attracted many manufacturing industries. The warm climate, number of workers available, and cheaper rent, power, and taxes have made the South an appealing place to do business.
- Coal mining is important in the mountain areas of the Appalachians. Coal is an important source of energy for heating. Coal mining produces many jobs in states such as Kentucky and West Virginia.
- The United States is one of the world's largest producers of petroleum and natural gas. Texas, Oklahoma, and Louisiana are leading petroleum and natural gas producers.
- Along the Atlantic Coast, textile production is important. North Carolina is one of the country's largest textile producers, making clothing, sheets, and towels. Other states, such as South Carolina, Alabama, and Georgia, also produce many textile products.
- Industries are supported by a highly developed transportation system. Highways, waterways, and railways allow for inexpensive ways of transporting goods.

Tourism Facts

- Nashville, home of the Grand Ole Opry, attracts country and western music fans. Louisville, Kentucky, attracts people to its famous horse race, the Kentucky Derby.
- New Orleans in Louisiana is the oldest city in the South, founded by the French in 1718. Many of the descendants have a mixed French and Spanish background, giving the city a unique culture. Once a year, it holds a huge party called Mardi Gras.

Agriculture Facts

- The climate is ideal for growing tobacco, cotton, soybeans, sweet potatoes, peanuts, rice, and sugar cane. In the subtropical climate of Florida, tomatoes, strawberries, and citrus fruit such as oranges and grapefruits are grown.
- Texas is second only to Alaska in land area. It is home to some of the biggest cattle ranches. There are more cattle than people in Texas!

Florida, often referred to as the Sunshine State, is one of the fastest growing states. Its warm temperatures and sandy beaches make it popular with tourists, too — including many Canadians!

SOMETHING TO DO

1. Continue your map-making of the United States by creating a map of the Southern Region. Identify major cities. Create symbols to represent industry, agriculture, and tourism features associated with the region. Place the symbols on the map and create a legend to identify what they represent.

WESTERN REGION

This region includes states bordering the Rocky Mountains as well as those along the Pacific Coast. In addition to the Rockies, this rugged region contains deserts, plains, plateaus, and river canyons. The Grand Canyon is probably the most famous canyon in the west.

Natural hazards, such as earthquakes and volcanoes, are no strangers to this region. California lies along the San Andreas fault. Here, two parts of the earth's crust meet and shift, causing frequent earthquakes.

Because this region is so large, it has many unique climatic conditions. The states of Washington and Oregon have rainy, cool weather. California has a warmer and sunnier climate. Some parts of California, Nevada, and Arizona can be very hot.

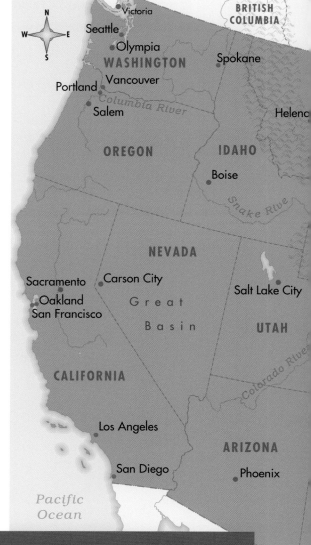

Industry Facts

- The Rocky Mountains are a storehouse of precious metals such as gold, silver, and copper. Mineral deposits are still harvested today in the states along the Rocky Mountains.
- The Pacific coastal states of Washington and Oregon are known for their dense forests. One-quarter of the country's timber is harvested from these two states.
- Oklahoma is one of the leading producers of natural gas and petroleum. In addition, oil is found in Montana and North Dakota.
- California is an industrial powerhouse and a leader in computer technology.

Agriculture Facts

- Many crops can be grown in California because of the ideal climate conditions. Oranges, nuts, vegetables, and cotton are just a few of the crops grown.
- In Washington and Oregon, the cool, wet climate is ideal for growing fruits and vegetables. Apples, raspberries, pears, apricots, and cherries are exported from this region to Canada.
- In the states surrounding the Rocky Mountains, mountain meadows provide grazing land for beef and dairy herds. Cattle and sheep farming are important in Montana, Wyoming, and Utah.
- Valleys spreading out from the mountains provide ideal conditions for growing crops. Wheat, barley, rye, oats, sugar beets, and potatoes are important crops.

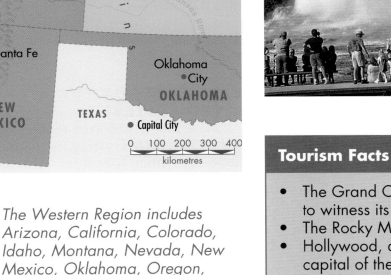

Yellowstone National Park, which lies mostly in Wyoming, is famous throughout the world for its geyser and hot springs. The most famous geyser, Old Faithful, erupts every 65 minutes.

The Western Region includes Arizona, California, Colorado, Idaho, Montana, Nevada, New Mexico, Oklahoma, Oregon, Utah, Washington, and Wyoming.

Tourism Facts

- The Grand Canyon is a natural wonder attracting millions to witness its splendour.
- The Rocky Mountains provide tourists with fantastic skiing.
- Hollywood, a section of Los Angeles, is the entertainment capital of the United States and the movie capital of the world.

SOMETHING TO DO

1. Continue your map-making of the United States by creating a map of the Western Region. Identify major cities. Create symbols to represent industry, agriculture, and tourism features associated with the region. Place the symbols on the map and create a legend to identify what they represent.

2. The Western Region is a major earthquake zone. Why do you think people want to live in this area in spite of the earthquakes?

Our trade relationship with the United States goes back a long time. Trade with the US began even before Canada became a country. Over the years, trade has increased between the two countries. In the 1980s, Canada and the United States got together to discuss a special trade relationship. The result was the Free Trade Agreement. The purpose of this agreement was to increase imports and exports between the two countries and to eliminate trade **tariffs**. A tariff is a tax on imported goods. The tax is added on to the regular price of the goods, making them more expensive.

Prime Minister Brian Mulroney signs the North American Free Trade Agreement.

NAFTA

In 1994, another trade agreement was signed. The North American Free Trade Agreement (NAFTA) not only further reduced the **trade barriers** between Canada and the United States, but brought Mexico into the agreement. Trade barriers are rules that are put in place by governments that sometimes make it difficult for countries to trade.

In 1994, not everyone agreed that NAFTA was a good thing. Many people believed it would do more harm than good to Canadians and the Canadian economy. Today, however, the agreement has made North America one of the richest markets in the world. The amount of trade between the three countries is five times greater than it was 20 years ago. The North American market has prospered and remained strong due to NAFTA.

DEPENDENCY ON THE UNITED STATES

In 2000, Canada exported more than $359 billion worth of merchandise to the United States. In turn, it exported more than $267 billion worth of goods to Canada.

Canada exports as much to the United States as the Americans export to Canada. The difference is that the amount Canada sends to the United States is 86 per cent of all Canadian exports. This percentage makes us extremely dependent upon the Americans. We need them to buy our goods and services.

Even though the United States sends an equal amount of trade to Canada, it is only 23 per cent of what the country exports in total. The United States is so large that it produces many goods and services. It relies on many countries to buy these goods and services.

Trading with the US

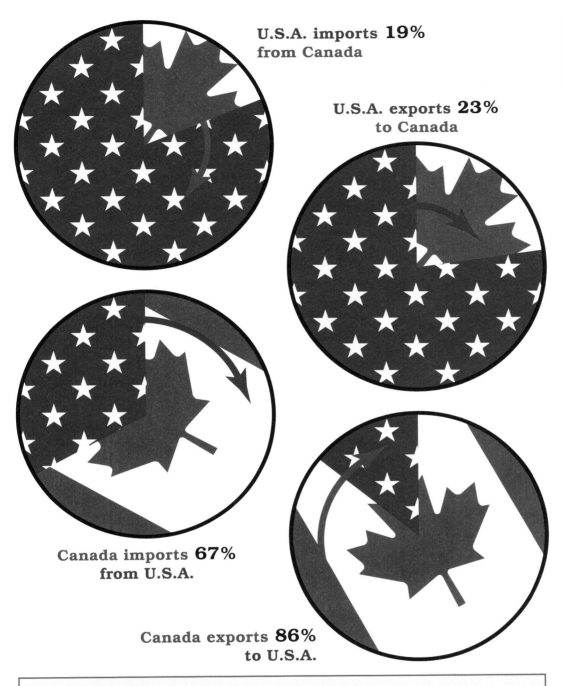

U.S.A. imports **19%** from Canada

U.S.A. exports **23%** to Canada

Canada imports **67%** from U.S.A.

Canada exports **86%** to U.S.A.

DID YOU KNOW?

The United States is a leading producer of:

- petroleum and natural gas
- coal
- synthetic rubber
- cement
- computers and electronic equipment
- paper
- non-electric machinery
- transportation equipment
- food and food products
- manufactured metal products
- chemicals and related products

SOMETHING TO DO

1. Interview an adult about free trade. Write down questions for the interview, such as:

   - Do you think Canada is better off with free trade? Why?

   - In what ways does the United States have more influence on Canada as a result of free trade?

   - What are some of the positive effects of free trade for Canadians? What are some of the negative effects?

   Take notes while you conduct your interview. Share your findings with a small group. Based on the group's findings, list the positive and negative views that were expressed by the people interviewed.

WHAT IS TRADED?

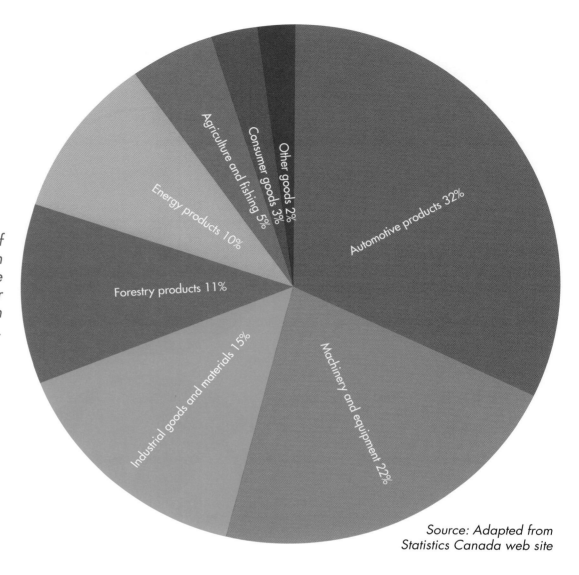

Automotive products 32%

Machinery and equipment 22%

Industrial goods and materials 15%

Forestry products 11%

Energy products 10%

Agriculture and fishing 5%

Consumer goods 3%

Other goods 2%

The majority of Canadians live within 100 km of the Canada/US border (80 per cent within 160 km).

Source: Adapted from Statistics Canada web site

WHY DO WE BUY AMERICAN?

There are benefits to having the United States as a neighbour, especially when it comes to fresh produce. Fruits and vegetables grow during the winter months in the warm climates of the southern states. Most of Canada during the winter is blanketed in snow. Fresh produce can be shipped quickly and easily from the southern states to Canada. Therefore we enjoy things such as fresh tomatoes, strawberries, oranges, and grapes all year round.

The similarities between the two countries is another reason Cana-dians love to buy American goods. Our taste in clothes, toys, music, and entertainment is similar to the tastes and likes of Americans. We buy many American products because they appeal to our tastes.

Easy access means citizens from both countries can cross the border to shop. Many American cities, such as Buffalo, New York, offer Canadian money at par to encourage Canadians to shop there. In other words, they will accept a Canadian dollar as being worth the same amount as an American dollar. This can be a real savings when the Canadian dollar is worth, say, 65¢ to $1 US!

*Many Canadians cross the border on weekends to shop in US cities like Buffalo, New York. In the busy summer months, they may have a long wait getting through **customs**.*

SOMETHING TO DO

1. Do you know more about Canada or the United States? Let's find out. Complete this quiz!

   Create a t-chart. On the left-hand column write the title "Canada." On the right-hand column write the title "The United States." For each country, provide one example of the following:

an inventor	a movie produced in that country
a politician	a capital city
an athlete	a medical discovery
a scientist	a news announcer
an author	a stock market
a sports team	a dancer
a musician	a lake
a technological wizard	a mountain range
a TV program	

   When you have completed the quiz, examine your results. Think, pair, and share in small groups to discuss reasons for the results.

2. Create a list of unique things about Canada that makes this country different from the United States. (You may want to ask an adult for ideas.) How important are each of these unique features to you? Which one would you want to make sure Canada never loses? Rank the features in order from "the most" to "the least" important to you.

3. Use an almanac to discover the total amount of trade between the United and five other countries. Create a bar graph to display the data. What conclusions can you draw about the amount of trade between the United States and these countries?

apan is a small country located in the Pacific Ocean. It is made up of four main islands — Hokkaido, Shikoku, Kyushu, and Honshu — and more than 3000 smaller islands.

Nearly two-thirds of Japan is covered in forests located on steep mountains. Most people live on the flatter, coastal plains.

Earthquakes, volcanoes, and tidal waves create havoc in Japan every year. There are 250 volcanoes, many of which are active. Ten per cent of the world's volcanoes are located in Japan.

In the north, winters are harsh and snowy. Summers are mild. In the south, winters are milder, but summers are hot and humid with a lot of rain. For three months of the year, this area is threatened with typhoons or tropical storms.

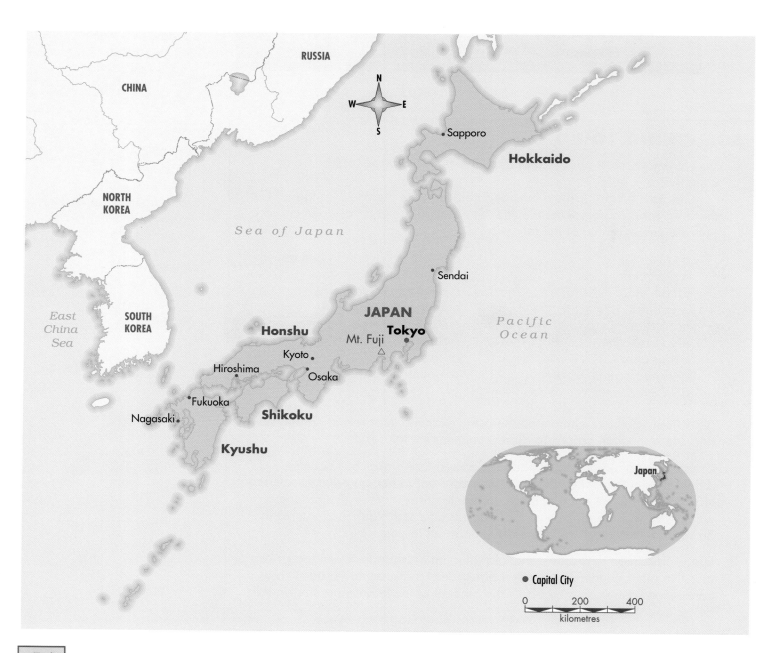

Japan: A Closer Look

Japan's most famous peak, Mount Fuji, is located on the island of Honshu.

Earthquakes have caused serious damage in Japan. This expressway that links the cities of Kobe and Osaka collapsed following a powerful earthquake in January 1995. Over 600 people were killed in the quake.

SOMETHING TO DO

1. Canada is more than 25 times larger than Japan. But Japan's population is four times greater than Canada's. There are a lot more people living per square kilometre in Japan than in Canada. How would this affect daily life in Japan? Consider traffic, parks, etc.

2. Do some research to find information on natural disasters that have occurred in Japan. Choose one disaster and make a brief presentation about it to the class. When organizing the information, consider "what, where, when, and why."

POLITICAL FACTS

- Until 1939, Japan was a prosperous and advanced nation, ruled by emperors. The emperor was usually a military ruler and a very powerful man. The position of emperor was inherited. From generation to generation, the job was passed down from father to son.
- After being defeated in World War II (1939-1945), Japan was a devastated country. Due to the war, Japanese people had lost their crops, houses, businesses, and factories. Many people were starving. The United States and other countries helped rebuild Japan into a democratic country.
- Today, although Japan still has an emperor, he has no political or military power. The Japanese government is similar to Canada's. Japan has a constitution, just like we do, that tells how the country should be run. There are several political parties that have different ideas of how the country should function. The people vote to elect the party they want to lead the country. The leader of the party becomes the prime minister. The prime minister has a cabinet that offers advice. The cabinet makes up part of the parliament, or as it is called in Japan, the Diet. The Diet is a group of elected officials from all parties that passes new laws.

SOCIAL FACTS

- Many homes are a blend of old and new ways. High-tech gadgets such as televisions and electronic games are found in many Japanese homes. There is often European-style furniture in addition to Japanese furniture. You will find many traditional items such as straw mats, called *tatami*, on which people often sit. There are also *futons*, which are mattresses placed directly on the floor. The futons, or beds, are rolled up and put away during the day.
- Many people in Japan today live in apartments built with the latest earthquake-proof technologies.

Homes in Japan blend modern high technology with traditional furnishings. Look at this photo and identify one piece of traditional Japanese furniture and one piece of modern technology.

Japan: A Closer Look

Like people in many countries, the Japanese enjoy American fast foods. Outlets like McDonald's are found in most Japanese cities.

- Most people live in cities, close to their businesses. A "city lifestyle" is very common in Japan.
- Many people in Japan work six days a week. They work many hours each day. Recently, there has been a move towards a shorter work week, meaning people would work fewer hours.
- Trade and the building of relationships with other countries has an impact on the Japanese culture. If you walk down the street of any Japanese city you will see the influence of Western culture. Almost everyone wears Western clothes and many of their favourite bands and pop stars are North American. You wouldn't have a hard time finding a McDonald's restaurant or seeing a baseball game in Japan!

DID YOU KNOW?

Japanese children attend school 240 days a year, with only six weeks of vacation. A typical school year in Canada is 190 days. Students attend school Monday to Friday as well as half of Saturday, with several hours of homework given each day. Students are taught to respect their teachers and to look after their school. The students and teachers are responsible for cleaning bathrooms, classrooms, and hallways.

Even with such a busy school schedule, children still find time for sports. Most children practise some type of martial arts, and baseball is played at school.

SOMETHING TO DO

1. Compare and contrast the interior of a typical Japanese home with a Canadian one.

2. Imagine you are going to interview a person your own age who lives in Japan. Create a list of questions that you might ask this person about his or her life in Japan.

JAPAN'S ECONOMY

Japan has grown to be one of the wealthiest and most technologically advanced countries in the world. It's a world leader in the production of cars, machinery, and electronics. If you play computer games, the hardware or software may have been made in Japan. The cartoons you watch on TV may have been produced in Japan. You may find many things in your house that are "Made in Japan."

The United States is Japan's largest trading partner. Thirty per cent of its manufactured goods are exported to the United States. Japan makes 11 million cars, trucks, and buses each year. The United States and Western Europe are the best customers for these automotive products.

Adapting to World Needs

Japan has always adapted to world needs. In the 1950s and 1960s, Japan focused on heavy industries. It produced steel, cement, and chemical products. When the cost of raw materials started to increase, Japan made a switch. It started to import raw materials to make products such as automobiles, cameras, and electronics. These products were cheaper to produce.

Japanese products are known all over the world. Cars, electronic equipment, cameras, and automobiles are made by well-known companies such as Sony, Toyota, and Kawasaki. Nearly all of the electronic goods around the world contain some Japanese parts. Other giant industries include steel, heavy machinery, chemicals, and shipbuilding. Some inventions include the transistor and the computer chip.

To make up for the lack of resources, Japan developed a strong economy based on manufacturing. The country is heavily dependent on importing raw materials, especially oil. Materials such as copper, coal, iron, lead, nickel, cotton, wool, wood, and rubber are also imported. The materials are then used to manufacture goods such as ships, cars, motorcycles, cameras, computers, televisions, stereo equipment, and musical instruments. These products are in turn exported. Japan pays for all of the materials it imports through the sale of the goods it exports.

These Japanese women are working on a production line making televisions. Japan is well known for its electronic products. What products does your family own that were made in Japan?

Japan: A Closer Look

High-tech industries employ many people in Japan. These industries include companies that manufacture computers, cameras, and other electronic equipment. The use of robotics in manufacturing has allowed companies to employ fewer people to run the business. People who once worked in manufacturing are now working in the service industry. These service jobs are in the areas of research, communications, and banking.

Trade with Canada

Japan is a large foreign investor in Canada. Japanese companies have purchased land and built manufacturing plants in Canada. Tourism is another source of trade between the two countries. More people come from Japan to visit Canada than from any other country in the world.

The Japanese automaker Honda developed this robot in 2000. What do you think robots could be used for?

Japan Exports to Canada ($11 billion of products)	Canada Exports to Japan ($9 billion of products)
• automobiles	• lumber
• power turbines	• wood pulp
• auto parts	• coal
• computers	• fish and seafood
• complex tools	• copper and aluminum
• iron and steel	• canola (used for cooking oil)

Source: Japanese Embassy in Canada Web site, 2000

SOMETHING TO DO

1. Working with a partner, examine the photos in this chapter on Japan.

   a) Pick the photo that most interests you. Explain to your partner why this photo interests you.

   b) Identify and discuss elements about the Japanese culture reflected in the photos.

 exico is the the thirteenth largest country in the world. A part of North America, it lies immediately south of the United States. The Rio Grande River forms a good part of the border between Mexico and the United States.

Mexico is a country of diverse landforms. Three mountain ranges that form a giant "V" run down one side of Mexico and back up the other. All three ranges are named Sierra Madre.

Mexico has two large **peninsulas**. Peninsulas are large tracts of land that have water on three sides. The Yucatan Peninsula forms the eastern side of Mexico. There are jungles within this peninsula. On the western side is the Baja California Peninsula. High mountains and dry desert make up this peninsula.

The climate varies greatly from one area of Mexico to the next. The climate is partially determined by the **altitude**. The altitude is measured by calculating the distance above sea level. **Sea level** is where the ocean meets the land. Those areas with the highest altitude in Mexico have a colder climate. Here, it is not unusual

Mexico

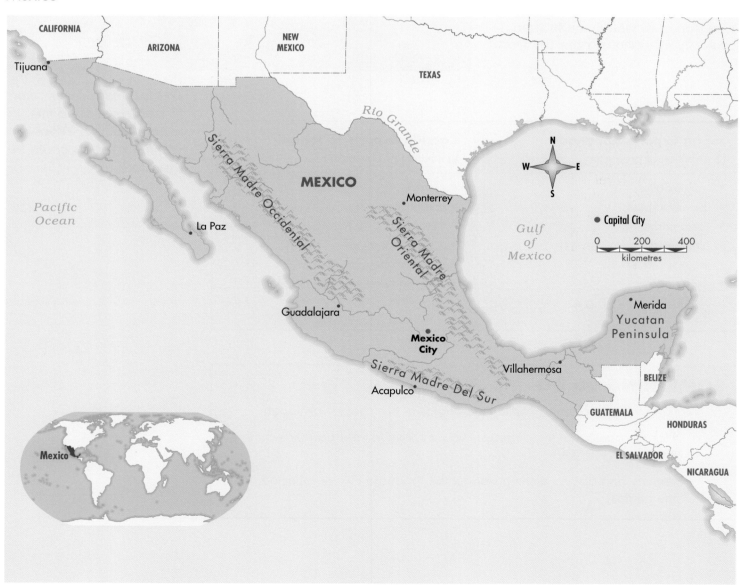

to have frost, and the mountain peaks are often snow-covered. The area below this level (910 to 1800 m above sea level) is where most crops are grown. It has a moderate to warm climate. The temperature usually stays between 10° and 27°C.

The area below 910 m has long, hot summers and mild winters.

Many areas in Mexico receive little rainfall. The northern part of Mexico is particularly dry. Only mountainous regions receive enough rainfall to grow crops.

The photo on the left shows the white beaches and blue waters of the Yucatan Peninsula.
The photo on the right shows the rugged hills and scrub brush of the Baja Peninsula.

SOMETHING TO DO

1. On the map of Mexico, locate all of the physical features described here.

POLITICAL FACTS

- Mexico is a federal republic. It has an executive branch, which is headed by a president. The executive branch is a group of politicians that makes decisions about laws, taxes, and policies within Mexico. There are 31 states. Each state has an elected governor and legislature.
- The president is elected for six years. For almost 70 years, the *Partido Revolucionario Institucional* party was in power. There were often rumours of **corruption** and poor leadership. In 1999, the PRI finally lost an election and a new party came into power.
- The government faces some big challenges in the twenty-first century. It needs to create jobs and build a strong economy.

SOCIAL FACTS

- Family life, holidays, and festivals are important to the Mexican people. Canada and Mexico share many of the same holidays, including Christmas, Easter, and Labour Day.
- In Mexico, education is free and children must attend school until they are 15. Mexico has many fine universities, technological institutes, and teachers' colleges for those who are able to pursue higher education.
- Mexico is rich in culture and is home to many artists. Art is a very important part of the Mexican culture. Today, every region produces some type of arts and crafts. Many of the art techniques date back thousands of years. Several of the art pieces are sold to tourists.

Mexico City is the largest city in the world with a population of 24 million.

- For many Mexicans who live in rural areas on farms, both parents work hard in the fields. Women are expected to work in the fields as well as look after the children and household. Women in the city have less traditional roles and often have jobs outside the home.
- Seventy-five per cent of the Mexican population lives in cities and towns. There are more people in the cities than there are jobs. Without jobs, many people live in poverty. Seventy per cent of the people are poor.
- The minimum wage for a worker is 18 pesos a day. This is not much considering a taco might sell on the street for 3 or 4 pesos and a McDonald's Big Mac, fries, and milk shake cost 16 pesos (almost a day's wage).
- Only a small percentage of the population makes a good wage. People are either extremely poor or extremely rich, with few people earning a middle-class income. The gap between the very wealthy and the very poor has grown much wider in the past decade.

Mexican crafts, such as pottery, are important sources of income for local artists and their communities.

Mexico City is a modern urban centre filled with office buildings, shops, restaurants, and cars. Yet not far away, on the outskirts of Mexico City, many people live in the traditional ways.

SOMETHING TO DO

1. Using a web organizer, list possible topics you could research that would make you more of an expert on Mexico. Under each topic, record some questions you would invesitgate.

Tourism is an important part of Mexico's economy. Many tourists come for the sun, sand, and ocean. But others come to explore Mexico's rich cultural heritage. This is a sacrificial altar at Chicen-Itza in the Yucatan Peninsula.

MEXICO'S ECONOMY

Until the 1950s, Mexico's economy relied on mining and farming. Then a shift towards more manufacturing took place. Today, Mexico manufactures many of the goods it uses.

In the 1970s, Mexico became a major exporter of petroleum to the United States. The money from petroleum sales was used to start up new manufacturing industries.

Mexico City produces about half of all of Mexico's goods. Monterey and Guadalajara are also important manufacturing centres. Chief manufacturing products include automobile engines and transmissions, stereo systems, computers, televisions, and kitchen appliances.

Mexico is famous for its silver. Many beautiful vases, jewellery, and cutlery are made from the silver it mines. Other exports include crude oil, oil products, coffee, engines, and cotton.

Service industries provide 50 per cent of the jobs in Mexico. There are more Mexicans employed in jobs related to tourism than in any other type of job. Tourists stay in hotels and eat in restaurants that hire Mexican workers. Tourists also spend money, which contributes significantly to Mexico's economy.

Mexico is also a source of cheap labour for many companies. A worker in Mexico might make $6 a day doing the same job as a worker in the United States who makes $6 an hour.

The United States is Mexico's largest trading partner, followed by the European Union and Japan. Mexico is looking to expand its trading partners in order to become less dependent upon the US.

Silver mining is an important industry in Mexico. The city of Taxco in central Mexico is known as the silver capital of the world.

NAFTA

The United States and Canada have had a successful trading relationship for many years. In 1991, the United States looked to its other neighbour, Mexico, to see if it could improve trade relations. When Canada learned of this new partnership, it decided to join them. At the time Canada traded little with Mexico. But losing some of American business to Mexico, or allowing the United States and Mexico to become a strong trading force, would not have benefitted Canada. As a result, negotiations between the three countries began.

There were many benefits to reaching an agreement. Between the three countries, there are 390 million people to both produce and buy goods. As well, the three countries working together make North America more powerful and competitive with Asian and European trade organizations.

Unfortunately, soon after the North American Free Trade Agreement was signed, Mexico experienced economic problems. The value of their currency, the peso, dropped. The peso was worth less and Mexicans had to pay more pesos for the same merchandise.

Since then, Mexico's economy has regained some strength. It is expected, however, that Mexico will continue to experience economic ups and downs while its economy expands and grows.

Canada Exports to Mexico	Mexico Exports to Canada
• motor vehicle parts	• motor vehicle parts
• wheat	• electronics
• canola	• appliances
• iron and steel products	• petroleum
• machinery and mechanical appliances	• engines
• telecommunications equipment	• data processing machines
• meat and livestock	• furniture
• paper and wood pulp	• edible fruits
• seeds	• nuts
• aircraft and parts	• vegetables
• dairy products	• glass and glassware and optical equipment

Source: *Curriculum Source Guides, Canada and Its Trading Partners* (Mississauga: MOD Publications, 1999).

SOMETHING TO DO

1. Spanish is Mexico's national language. Here are some common Spanish terms you might need to know if you were to visit Mexico.

English	Spanish
Good morning	*Buenos dias*
How are you?	*Como esta usted?*
Thank you	*Gracias*
Good-bye	*Adios*

   If you were travelling to Mexico on business, what other terms might you need to know?

2. Compare the amount of trade we do with the United States with the amount of trade we do with Mexico. Do you think the amount of trade we do determines the amount of influence a country has on us? Are there other factors that determine how great the influence is?

o you remember the story of Brenden, Hannah, and David? Each of them was responsible for contributing goods and services to create the final product, the lemonade.

Not long ago, it was easy to identify a product as Canadian, or German, or Japanese. That is not true anymore. Often large corporations offer the jobs of design, production, marketing, and distribution to businesses and factories in a variety of countries. Corporations will look for countries that are either good at a certain aspect of production, such as advertising, or that offer a service at a low cost. A lower cost will hopefully ensure greater sales and increased profits.

Let's take a look at the steps involved in getting a product from the design stage to the store shelves. Imagine a product such as a soft drink.

- The actual idea for a new drink might come from a food company in Canada. This is the research and design component of product development.
- The raw materials might come from several countries, depending on the ingredients. Cocoa might be imported from Colombia and sugar might be imported from Jamaica. The drink might then be produced at a manufacturing plant in Mexico where labour is cheaper. This is the production stage.
- A company from Germany might do the advertising.
- It might be packaged in the United States and shipped from there to other countries.

Many countries will have been responsible for the making of this new drink.

RESEARCH

The first thing researchers need to do is establish the market—that is, who the consumers, or buyers, are going to be. Then they can determine what these customers want and the price they are willing to pay. They need to know what is popular since this affects what consumers will want to buy.

DESIGN

A good designer will look at all of the possibilities involving materials, design, colours, and so on for the new product. From these possibilities, he or she will create a few models or samples. In developing the product, a designer needs to keep in mind the cost of materials since the final cost cannot be more than the price consumers are willing to pay. In addition, the designer must ensure that the product is safe and able to hold up to reasonable use.

ADVERTISING AND PROMOTION

Advertising includes television commercials, print advertisements, catalogues, displays, and promotions. The ad campaign must be appropriate for intended customers and must be ready as soon as the product hits the market.

PRODUCTION

Raw materials are gathered and used to make the product. Goods are either made by hand or by machine. Most products today are made by machines, which may be operated by computers. Manufacturing the product often requires skilled workers. The company will want to keep manufacturing costs as low as possible.

Insights into Production

PACKAGING

The packaging of a product has to take several factors into account. It has to be appealing to customers so that they will want to buy the product. Information about the product needs to be included on the packaging as well. It also has to be sturdy enough so that the product isn't damaged during shipping.

SHIPPING AND DISTRIBUTION

The product might be shipped by road, rail, air, or sea to its intended markets. The means of shipping must be appropriate to the product. For example, some products might need refrigeration so they don't spoil while in transport.

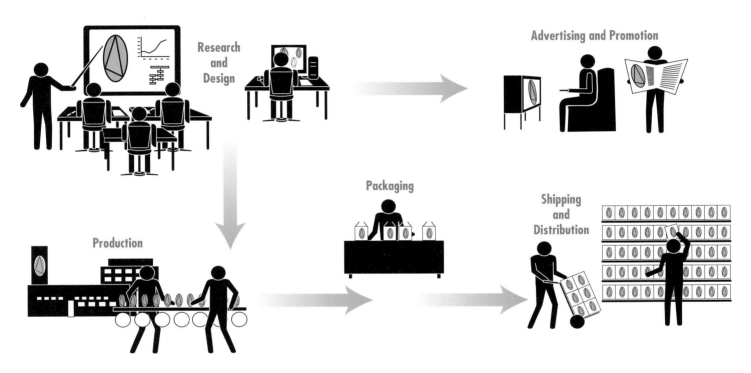

Steps in Developing and Producing a Product

SOMETHING TO DO

1. Work in groups of four or five students to create a new product, for example, a new chocolate bar, popcorn, ice cream, etc.

   a) Survey your class or other classes to determine favourite features of your product. Let's say that you chose chocolate bars as your product. Conduct a survey to find out what students like about chocolate bars.

   b) Based on the survey results, start creating your new product. Research countries that might supply your main ingredients, the work force, etc.

   c) What will be the cost of your product? What is the current cost of the item on the market?

   d) Design attractive packaging and advertising materials. Give your product a name. Present your new product to the class.

 any Canadians have made unique contributions to the global community. Here are just a few of the people who have earned a place in the international spotlight.

DONOVAN BAILEY

Donovan Bailey was born in Jamaica in 1967. He moved to Canada at the age of 13. He attended high school in Oakville, Ontario, and graduated from Sheridan College in marketing. In Toronto, as he was building a successful career in the financial area, he ran track as a hobby. His "hobby" led him to set a world record in the 100 m race and become a double champion at the 1996 Olympics. He was also a three-time World Champion.

CLAUDIA BERTRAND

In 1998, the Royal Canadian Mint launched the Create a Centsation Millennium Coin Design Contest. The challenge was to design a coin that celebrated an event in Canadian history or illustrated Canada's hope for the future. Over 60 000 entries from Canadians of all ages were received. One of the entries selected came from 10-year-old Claudia Bertrand of Beauport, Quebec. Her design, called "Canada Through A Child's Eye," is a drawing of three people holding hands representing family, friendship, and sharing. Her design appeared on the September 1999 coin. This accomplishment made her the youngest person ever to design a Canadian coin.

ROBERTA BONDAR

Roberta Bondar was the first Canadian woman in space. Born in Sault Ste. Marie, Ontario, she has a science background and is a doctor of medicine. Aboard the space shuttle *Discovery* in 1992, Bondar carried out 43 different experiments that examined how things behaved while weightless. During the mission she grew seedlings and tested the hand-eye co-ordination and balance of the other astronauts. The information she gathered was not only helpful for future missions, but had the possibility of further advancing stroke research.

WESLEY CHU

Eight-year-old Calgary pianist Wesley Chu is no stranger to audiences. Wesley gave his first piano performance at the age of three. By the time he was five, he had passed all nine grades of the Royal Conservatory of Music program. Since that first concert, he has played before Pope John Paul II and Queen Elizabeth II, played with Calgary's Philharmonic Orchestra, and appeared on the Rosie O'Donnell and Bill Cosby shows. People marvel at his incredible skill and talent. Some have compared him to Mozart. Today, Wesley writes his own music and has recorded his first CD.

CELINE DION

Celine Dion is just one of many artists who have helped put Canada on the international music scene. Born in Quebec, and the youngest of 13 children, Celine was popular in her home province before she was known in the rest of Canada or the United States. During her early singing career, all of her songs were performed in French. Deciding to expand her audience, she cut her first English album in 1990. Although it produced four hits, it was not until she sang the title song for the hit movie *Beauty and the Beast* that she started to gain an international audience. Celine has won both Grammy and Juno awards. Today, she is recognized around the world for her music, powerful voice, and genuine personality.

15

KAREN KAIN

Born in Hamilton, Ontario, Karen Kain enrolled in the National Ballet School at the young age of 11. After graduating, she began dancing with the National Ballet. In just one year, she became a principal dancer. Soon Karen was performing major ballet roles for audiences all over the world. She and her frequent partner, Frank Augustyn, won many international awards, ranking her as one of the world's finest dancers.

CRAIG KIELBURGER

When he was 12, Craig Kielburger read a newspaper report about a child who had been sold into slavery by his parents and was eventually murdered. The child was murdered because he had been working to free other children from being forced to work. Deeply touched by the article, Craig set out on a seven-week trip to South Asia to find out for himself the conditions of working children. Appalled at what he saw, he started to speak out against child labour. Together with several of his friends, he founded the organization, Free the Children. It now has 20 chapters around the world.

KEITH PEIRIS

Keith Peiris is like most teenagers. He loves to play on the computer. The only difference with Keith is that he has been able to turn his "play" into a business. Keith's business is building Web sites for companies. Using a computer software program called Macromedia, he incorporates animated graphics with sound to produce pages that can be downloaded quickly. How does a 12-year-old person run a successful business? The business is run out of his parents' basement where five other part-time and full-time employees work. Keith himself puts in five hours a day after homework and between hockey games. How successful is his business? Very! His business, Cyberteks Design, is considered one of the top 50 Web site design companies in Canada. It has won dozens of awards.

Canadians on the World Stage

DAVID SUZUKI

David Suzuki is an award-winning scientist, environmentalist, and broadcaster. For over 30 years he has educated people about the workings of the world through programs such as *The Nature of Things*. A passionate speaker when it comes to the Earth's fragile environment, he has raised the environmental awareness of millions of people around the world. David Suzuki is involved in many worldwide organizations that help protect the planet. His documentary *A Planet For the Taking* won an award from the United Nations.

MORGAN LONG

At the age of 12, Morgan Long was preparing for an art show featuring her paintings. An art gallery in Italy had invited her to display 25 of her works, which included both abstract and realistic paintings.

Morgan started to paint at a young age. She was drawing cartoon characters before she turned three. At the age of 11, she drew a falcon. It won a contest and was used as an illustration on a greeting card. Everyone thought the falcon was the work of the famous wildlife painter Robert Bateman!

Today, Morgan paints three hours each day during the week and for most of the weekend. Her dream is to one day have her paintings displayed in galleries throughout the world.

SOMETHING TO DO

1. Select a Canadian who has made a contribution to our country or to the global community. Dramatize one important event from his or her life.

2. Cut out pictures from magazines and create a collage to illustrate the variety of contributions Canadians have made in the fields of science, art, drama, dance, business, etc.

What organizations do you or your family belong to? Are you part of a sports organization, a boys or girls club, or a member of a religious group? Why do you belong to the organization?

An organization is a group of people who meet for a specific purpose. Members of an organization usually have something in common. They may share religious beliefs, have the same interests, are of similar age or culture, or share common experiences. Usually an organization has a common goal. That goal might be to have fun together, or it may be of a more serious nature.

TRADE ORGANIZATIONS

Trade organizations include countries that have decided to work together to achieve a common goal. The goal may be to promote economic, social, political, or military co-operation among its members. Most importantly, trade organizations promote trade and economic growth.

Countries who are part of a trade organization will often agree to remove barriers in order to promote trade. You might recall that trade barriers are rules that are put in place by the governments of countries that sometimes make it difficult for countries to trade.

Adding tariffs, or extra taxes, to imported goods is one example of a trade barrier. A government places a tax on an imported product. This makes the cost higher than that of a similar product made at home. The tax makes it difficult for other countries to sell their products in that country.

The government can also impose a **quota**. This means there is a limit on the amount of that product that can come into a country. The United States and Canada have limited the numbers of cars and trucks that can be imported into North America. Not only are imported cars more expensive, but the customer may have to wait for an imported product to be available. Most people don't want to have to wait when buying a car!

Removing taxes and other trade barriers helps promote trade. When countries can trade freely and their product is not subjected to a tax or

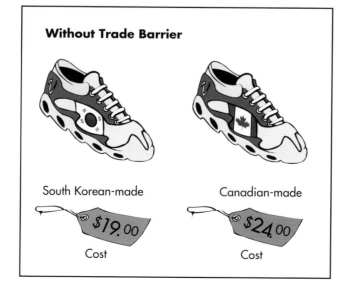

Without Trade Barrier

South Korean-made — $19.00 — Cost

Canadian-made — $24.00 — Cost

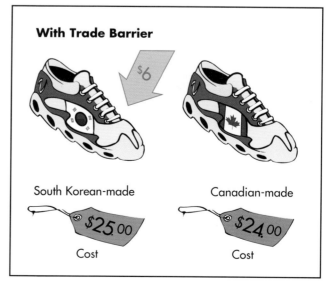

With Trade Barrier

$6

South Korean-made — $25.00 — Cost

Canadian-made — $24.00 — Cost

limited in number, it creates an **open market**.

Removing trade barriers between countries increases tolerance. Trade allows for the sharing of cultures and ideas between countries and breaks down the barriers between people.

TRADE AGREEMENTS

When you make a trade, how do you reach an agreement with your trading partner? How do you make sure that the agreement isn't broken? Most of your agreements are probably verbal. It is unlikely any of your agreements are in writing.

Countries that trade require a sophisticated type of agreement. Countries cannot afford to have other countries back out of deals. International agreements are written legal documents. What is going to be traded, how, where, when, and at what cost are just a few of the terms or conditions included in the contract. Both parties, or in this case countries, need to agree to the terms and to sign the agreement.

Trade agreements need to be legal documents in case a dispute occurs. In this way, a court can be used to help settle any problems.

Agreements are usually hammered out as a result of meetings in trade organizations. Trade agreements and organizations go hand in hand. It is not enough to sign an agreement and hope that trade will proceed smoothly. Organizations are necessary to monitor agreements, establish fair rules, and assist in settling disputes.

CANADA AND INTERNATIONAL TRADE

Canada is involved in world trade in a variety of ways. These include trade missions by Canadian political and business leaders, participation in trade-related organizations, and memberships in world cultural organizations. The following are some of the ways in which Canada pursues its international trade relations.

Team Canada

Political leaders, business leaders, and the prime minister of Canada have arranged several special tours in the past decade. This group is called *Team Canada*. The goal of their tours is to promote Canadian goods and services and to show the rest of the world that Canada is a stable and secure place to do business. They also promote arts, culture, and tourism.

Team Canada has travelled to several places around the world, developing a number of trade agreements. Further trade creates jobs and economic growth. The government boasts that the efforts

Team Canada, 2000

of Team Canada have resulted in over 880 deals in over 13 countries, with an estimated worth of approximately $25 billion.

THE WORLD TRADE ORGANIZATION (WTO)

The **World Trade Organization** was established in 1995. Today it has 137 members, including Canada. The WTO is the only international organization dealing with the rules of trade among nations. Its main tasks include:

- helping developing countries gain greater economic prosperity
- offering help in exporting
- arranging regional trade
- co-operating in global economic policymaking
- informing members of changes in trade policies.

THE ORGANIZATION FOR ECONOMIC COOPERATION AND DEVELOPMENT (OECD)

The purpose of the **Organization for Economic Cooperation and Development** is to promote world trade and to help solve economic problems. Most of the members of the OECD are among the wealthiest countries in the world. Canada has been a member since the organization was formed in 1961.

G-8

G-8, or the Group of Eight, meets regularly to discuss economic issues before they become sources of conflict. Members include Canada, the United States, Germany, France, Great Britain, Japan, Italy, and Russia.

Trade in the Asia Pacific Region

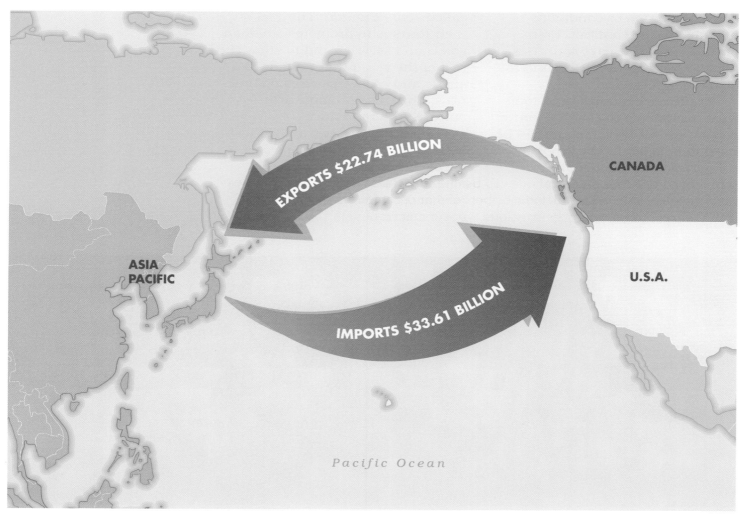

ASIA PACIFIC ECONOMIC COOPERATION (APEC)

The 21 member countries of the **Asia Pacific Economic Cooperation** border on the Pacific Ocean. The goal of the organization is to promote economic cooperation and freer trade and to promote economic growth among its members. Since it was formed in 1989, APEC has helped to establish the Asia-Pacific region as the fastest-growing economic region in the world.

THE COMMONWEALTH

Originally, membership in the **Commonwealth** was based on the colonial ties of the British Empire. Today, the Commonwealth is no longer based on political ties but on a cultural bond that unites 54 independent countries. These countries have a combined population of over 1.5 billion people. The key objective of the Commonwealth is to promote racial harmony and understanding. One aspect of this is to provide greater economic opportunities in developing countries. Trade is one way of supporting economic growth.

LA FRANCOPHONIE

La Francophonie was formed in 1960 as a forum for the French-speaking countries of the world. Today, representatives from 52 countries meet every two years to discuss the political, economic, and cultural issues that affect them. As a **bilingual** country, Canada is a member of la Francophonie. As a developed country, Canada has an important role to play in supporting economic growth in developing member countries.

ORGANIZATION OF AMERICAN STATES (OAS)

The **Organization of American States** was established in 1948 to promote peace and the economic development of the countries in the Western Hemisphere. The Western Hemisphere includes all of North and South America. As well as promoting trade, the OAS will defend any military attack on any American state. Countries work closely together to promote peace and discuss methods of combatting poverty, drugs, and corruption.

SOMETHING TO DO

1. List some of the organizations you belong to. What do you have in common with the rest of the members of that organization? What is your common goal? Why do you enjoy being a member?

2. a) Reflect on what trading rules you put into action when you make a trade. What do you do if a conflict arises?

   b) Role-play setting up a trade agreement between Canada and the United States to sell Canadian fresh water. Use some of the skills you discussed in a).

eacekeepers travel all over the world to countries engaged in a conflict. By the time peacekeepers enter a dispute, fighting is usually well under way. Peacekeepers are there to help save the lives of innocent people who are not fighting and to help the warring parties find a way to peacefully settle the dispute.

Peacekeepers come from different countries to be objective and act as referees. They are sent into the conflict to help find solutions to political disputes. Peacekeepers are not just soldiers but negotiators and diplomats.

DID YOU KNOW?

Prior to becoming prime minister of Canada in 1963, Lester B. Pearson headed the Canadian delegation to the United Nations. During his time at the UN, he acted as a **mediator** and negotiated an end to the **Suez Crisis** in 1956. Pearson won the Nobel Peace Prize in 1957 for his efforts.

The **United Nations** arranges most peacekeeping operations. The UN sends in **peacekeeping forces** only when both conflicting sides agree they want help settling the conflict. Many countries send soldiers to the United Nations peacekeeping missions. Since 1947, over 70 countries have sent men and women to peacekeeping missions. Over 600 000 soldiers have been involved in some type of mission.

CANADA'S PEACEKEEPING MISSIONS

Canada has been involved in peacekeeping missions for over 40 years. During those years, 120 000 Canadian soldiers have been sent to war-torn countries all over the world. Canada is the only country to have participated in almost every peacekeeping mission.

Canadian peacekeepers are experienced and have gained a great deal of expertise in resolving conflicts. Many countries looking to join the UN peacekeeping forces turn to Canada for advice.

Peacekeeping can be a dangerous job. Between 1947 and 1991, over 400 Canadians died on UN missions (314 in Korea). Often their jobs involve clearing mine fields and disposing of unexploded bombs. Sometimes peacekeepers, in their efforts to protect innocent civilians, get caught in the crossfire. They may even end up being held hostage.

PROBLEMS IN PEACEKEEPING

The efforts of the peacekeepers are not always appreciated. Often people expect that peacekeeping forces will be able to put an end to the war. This is not always the case, and although their mission is to help settle the dispute this is not always possible. Some conflicts are thousands of years old and people have been raised with certain beliefs and hostilities towards another group. These feelings are very hard to break. It may take years to make any headway.

Occasionally peacekeepers find themselves "between a rock and a hard place." Sometimes, they are accused by both sides of favouring the other side. It is difficult to negotiate peace if one or both sides mistrusts the negotiator. This

Lester B. Pearson

Canada's peacekeeping forces in Kosovo

becomes a no-win situation for the peacekeepers.

Maintaining world peace comes with a hefty price tag. The United Nations spends several million dollars each year to keep its peacekeeping missions going. This money comes from all countries. Unfortunately, not every country pays its full share, nor does it pay on time.

For some time, the United States refused to pay its share because it felt the United Nations was not using the money wisely. Canada is the fifteenth largest nation in population, and we are the fourth largest contributor to the United Nations. Canada always pays its full share on time.

DID YOU KNOW?

After World War II, countries got together to form an organization in the hope of preventing another world war. In 1945, 50 countries, including Canada, signed a proclamation vowing to "save succeeding generations from the **scourge** of war." The organization was called the United Nations.

Since that time, the United Nations has grown to include 187 countries. Each of these countries has a representative who presents his or her country's concerns to the **General Assembly**.

In addition to maintaining world peace, the UN also promotes cooperation among nations to help solve economic, cultural, social, and humanitarian problems.

SOMETHING TO DO

1. Do some research on Canada's role in peacekeeping. Refer to the following site: www.dfait–maeci.gc/peacekeeping

2. Many countries feel peacekeeping missions are becoming too expensive and are no longer effective at resolving conflicts. In a group, discuss whether peacekeeping missions should continue. Explore and discuss other means of resolving conflicts around the world.

Glossary

Altitude the height above sea level

APEC Asia Pacific Economic Co-operation—a group of countries bordering on the Pacific Ocean whose aim is to foster economic cooperation and development among its members

Archaeologists scientists who study history through ancient sites

Bartering trading by exchanging one good or service for another

Bilingual speaking two languages

Circumference the distance around a circle

Colonies countries or regions that are ruled by another country

Commonwealth an association of 54 countries that were once part of the British Empire that meet to promote economic equality, educational opportunities, and racial harmony

Consumers people who buy goods and services

Currency the money of a country

Customs the area at a border crossing or airport where government officials check passports and baggage

Developed country a country that is economically strong and industrialized

Developing country a country that is economically weak and where the majority of people lack education opportunities and adequate living conditions

Domestic products goods made within a country

Domestic trade trade that occurs between people in the same country

Economy a country's changing wealth that comes from the production, distribution, and consumption of goods and services

European Union the 15-member organization aimed at creating a united Europe; members as of March 2001 include Austria, Belgium, Denmark, Finland, France, Germany, Greece, Ireland, Italy, Luxembourg, the Netherlands, Portugal, Spain, Sweden, and Great Britain

Exports products or services that are sold to another country

Finished product a product that is complete

Foreign belonging outside of a place or country

Foreign aid money, food, and other resources given to one country by another

Foreign investment money invested in a country by a company in another country

Free trade the promotion of trade through the removal of trade barriers

General Assembly the main body of the United Nations

Global community the concept that the world is becoming interconnected in many way so that boundaries between countries are less important

Goods raw materials or manufactured consumer products

Greenwich Mean Time the local time at 0° longitude

Gross domestic product total value of goods and services a country produces in a year

Industry manufacturing and services

Immigration coming into a country or region to live

Imports products or services brought in from another country

International Date Line the line from north to south partly at 180° longitude

International trade trade that occurs between people in different countries

la Francophonie organization comprising 52 French-speaking countries that

gather to discuss common interests and promote development opportunities

Labour costs the amount a company pays its workers

Manufactured consumer goods something that promotes international trade made by hand or machine from raw materials

Mediator a person who works to resolve disputes between two or more parties

Middle East an area in western Asia and northern Africa stretching from the Mediterranean Sea to Pakistan

NAFTA North American Free Trade Agreement—an agreement signed by Canada, the United States, and Mexico to lower trade barriers and promote trade between the three countries

Natural resources materials harvested from nature for their usefulness, such as, timber, coal, and natural gas

Needs the things we have to have in order to meet our basic requirements for food, shelter, and clothing

Nomadic a way of life in which people roam from place to place in search of food or fresh pasture

Non-renewable natural resources

that cannot be replaced once they're consumed

OAS Organization of American States — a trade organization whose purpose is to promote peace and economic development in countries in the Western Hemisphere

On-line directly connected to a centre via computer

Open market a market in which countries can trade freely without taxes or trade barriers

Peacekeeping forces a part of the United Nations that consists of neutral soldiers, negotiators, and diplomats aimed at negotiating or maintaining peace and protecting citizens

Peninsula a piece of land almost surrounded by water

Prime Meridian the 0° line of longitude that passes through Greenwich, England

Products goods that are manufactured

Profits the amount of money earned after costs are deducted

Quota the amount of a product that is allowed

Raw materials materials in their natural form, such as timber, oil, and natural gas, that have not been changed to make other products

Renewable resources natural resources that nature can replenish, provided they are managed properly

Roman Empire the territories under Roman rule from 27 BCE to 476 CE

Sea level where the ocean meets the land

Scourge something that causes trouble or suffering

Services work performed by people for other people

Standard of living the quantity and quality of goods and services people in a country can buy

Suez Crisis the conflict that followed after Egypt took control of the Suez Canal

Supply and demand the number of items available and the number of people wanting them

Surplus an amount of something greater than the amount needed

Tax a monetary charge added to a product or service

Tariffs the combined taxes a country places on imports

Team Canada a group of Canadian political and business leaders, led by the prime minister, who promote Canadian goods and services abroad

Time zones the division of the world into 24 different regions for the purpose of creating a standard time within each region

Trade to buy, sell, or exchange goods and services

Trade agreements legal documents that describe the terms of trade between the trading parties

Trade barrier a tax or restriction intended to limit trade

Trade organizations groups of countries that work together to strengthen trade among their members

Trading partners at least two countries exchanging goods and services

United Nations an organization that promotes world peace and co-operation among nations and works to solve economic, social, political, and humanitarian problems

Wants the things we like to have but that we don't have to have in order to meet our basic needs

Work force employed people who produce goods and services

World Bank an organization affiliated with the United Nations that provides loans to developing countries

WTO World Trade Organization—an organization that establishes rules for trade in the global community

PHOTO CREDITS

t=top; b=bottom; c=centre; l=left; r=right

8 Wayne Shiels/VALAN PHOTOS; 9 Dick Hemingway; 11 Judy-Ann Cazemier/Ivy Images; 15 NAC/-002774; 18 (t) Ivy Images, (b) Charlene Daly/VALAN PHOTOS; 19 R. Moller/VALAN PHOTOS; 20 (l) Jean Bruneau/ VALAN PHOTOS, (r) Ivy Images; 24 (l) Wayne Shfer/ VALAN PHOTOS, (c) © Barrett & MacKay Photography Inc., (r) Dick Hemingway; 27 Michael Krasowitz/FPG International; 30 Mary C. Dixon/Ivy Images; 31 Yann Layma/Stone; 32 Jeff Greenberg/Ivy Images; 33 Adrian Arbib/CORBIS/MAGMA PHOTO; 35 John Cancalosi/VALAN PHOTOS; 36 (t) Ivy Images, (c) Dick Hemingway, (b) Tom Hanson/CP Picture Archive; 37 from top to bottom: Bill Becker/CP Picture Archive, © Barrett & MacKay Photography Inc., © Horizon International (Pat Lucero)/Ivy Images, Dick Hemingway; 41 Jean-Marie Jro/VALAN PHOTOS; 43 Jeff Greenberg/Ivy Images; 44-45 Wide World Inc./CP Picture Archive; 47 Bruce Hands/Stone; 49 First Light; 50 Frank Gunn/CP Picture Archive; 53 Ivy Images; 55 (t) Ivy Images, (b) AP Photo/CP Picture Archive; 56 Paul Chesley/Stone; 57 Jeff Greenberg/Ivy Images; 58 Charles Gupton/Stone; 59 AP Photo/CP Picture Archive; 61 (l) © Barrett & MacKay Photography Inc., (r) Aubrey Lang/VALAN PHOTOS; 62 Robert Frerck/ Stone; 63 all © Barrett & MacKay Photography Inc.; 64 (t) © Barrett & MacKay Photography Inc., (b) © Sergio Dorantes/CORBIS/MAGMA PHOTO; 68 (t) Paul Chiasson/CP Picture Archive, (bl) Canada News Wire/ Royal Canadian Mint/CP Picture Archive, (br) © 2001 Canadian Space Agency; 69 (t) Ken Kerr, Sun Media Corp., (b) Wide World Inc./CP Picture Archive; 70 (tl) Hans Deryk/CP Picture Archive, (tr) Tom Hanson/ CP Picture Archive, (b) Fred Chartrand/CP Picture Archive; 71 (t) Toronto Star-Rene Johnston/CP Picture Archive, (b) Courtesy of Morgan Long and OWL Magazine; 73 Fred Chartrand/CP Picture Archive; 76 CP Picture Archive; 77 AP Photo/CP Picture Archive

80